ZAMBIA SPORTING SCORE

MOSES SAYELA WALUBITA

iUniverse, Inc.
Bloomington

ZAMBIA SPORTING SCORE
A Period of Hits and Misses

First Published in Zambia in 1990

Pictures by Courtesy of Zambia Daily Mail

iUniverse books may be ordered through booksellers or by contacting:

iUniverse
1663 Liberty Drive
Bloomington, IN 47403
www.iuniverse.com
1-800-Authors (1-800-288-4677)

PHOTOS ON COVER:
TOP (from left) - Former Zambia's world 400 metres hurdles champion Samuel Matete in full flight; Soccer star Godfrey 'Ucar' Chitalu (behind) in a tussle for the ball; and Netball thrills in Lusaka.
BOTTOM (from left) – Zambian professional golfer Madaliso Muthiya; Zambia's All-Africa and Commonwealth light-heavyweight boxing champion Lottie Mwale (right); and Lawn tennis action in Zambia.

ISBN: 978-1-4502-7911-6 (sc)
ISBN: 978-1-4502-7912-3 (ebook)

Printed in the United States of America

iUniverse rev. date: 8/23/2011

Dedicated to my dear wife
Alice Siachika S. Walubita
and our late two sons.

TABLE OF CONTENTS

FOREWORD

Firstly, I would like to thank my dear comrade Moses Sayela Walubita for affording me an opportunity to write something in relation to sport and also to congratulate him for the brilliance and initiative in producing this valuable book. I have been closely associated with comrade Walubita in sports circles for a very long time. He is one those humble and dedicated young men. Our country is fortunate to have devoted young men like him who are able to contribute to the development of sport in Zambia.

The Party and its Government attaches great importance to sport. This is Because it is believed that meaningful development can only come about through Physical fitness among Zambians in tackling their day to day work, and this can on Be accomplished through sports promotion. However, for the development of sport in Zambia , organizers have incurred a lot of difficulties in, as far as, the promotion of sporting activities is concerned. This is due to the fact that sports development in the country is largely organized on voluntary basis.

Contribution through the writing of books is significant to any given situation because the information contained in the books so written remain a source of reference for future generations for a very long time, unlike in situations where we may have to rely on memory alone. Writing a book is therefore a difficult task. It requires a lot of research in order to gather the right facts.

To the potential readers, I am positive you will find this book of immense interest and educational value.

I wish comrade Walubita good luck and God's blessings in all his endeavours.

Mary K. Fulano (Mrs) M.C.C.
CHAIRMAN
YOUTH AND SPORTS COMMITTEE
LUSAKA
24 June, 1986

ACKNOWLEDGEMENT TO FIRST EDITION

I wish to acknowledge the tremendous support rendered by some sports associations and individuals in one way or another during the difficult moment of preparing this book.

Prominent among the many helpers are Barclays Bank (Zambia) Limited, Ridgeway Hotel, Guru Singh, Satwant Singh and Honda Zambia, who also helped financially in ensuring that the project took off. The book almost belongs to them. Thanks to Yusuf 'Pathan' Patel, David I. Stirk, FRCS, co-author of a book entitled 'The Compleat Golfer' in Britain, Zambia Motor Sports Association, Hiran Ray, Maxwell Sichula, Zambia Lawn Tennis Association and Zambia Polo Association for permission to quote their articles. To former Chairman of the Women's Affairs Committee. Mrs. Mary Fulano, Member of Party Central Committee, for accepting to write 'Foreword' even at short notice before she was transferred to the Women's Affairs Committee.

To Owen Phillips, Haroon Ghumra, Arnold Nyirenda, Pam Barker, Mary Bourne, Ngalama Kalaluka, Alf Francis, John Shamboko, Father Jude McKenna, Paul Luanga, Solly Patel, James Walubita, Mulenga Kapoka, Bill Chanda, John Mwale, Arthur Wina, Samson Mubangalala, Godfrey Mwanza, Mike Kabwe, Francis Sichande, Tony Robinson, Mwamba Kalenga, Desi McVeigh, Leslie McVeigh, Ian Fleming, Ravi Patel, Gool Muhammed Gool, Mrs. Mavis Muyunda, Mathew Zulu, Ridgeway Liwena, Derrick Mwenya, Jay Mwamba and Samuel Kasama.

Gerald Mwale for the service of his typewriter, Alan Wateridge for suggesting the main title to the book and going through part of the compilation. To Fred M'ule and Henry Mwakamui for editing the manuscript in their spare time. To my wife Alice Syamuyoba Walubita and our children

Walubita, Nambula, Sipakeli, Nalukui and Mwangala for enduring the endless cracking of typewriter sometimes late into midnight. To Emmah Naidu, Beauty Banda, Matilda Yasini and my cousin Inonge Sitali for typing the manuscript.

I had inspiration from Philip Chirwa and Mkwapatira Mhango. I am indebted to my brother Keli Walubita who first read the questionnaires sent to the National Associations. None of the above mentioned people but me, should be held responsible for any errors in the book.

To colleagues at the *Sachsiches Tageblatt* newspaper in Dresden, German Democratic Republic (GDR) and to the entire staff of the International Institute of Journalism /'Werner Lamberz' in Berlin. Thanks should also be extended to *Zambia Daily Mail* Management and several people who assisted me with the photographs, and to Multimedia (Zambia) Publishing Director Patrick Wele and Publishing Editor Mbuyu Nalumango for the co-operation.

ACKNOWLEDGEMENT TO SECOND EDITION

The long journey to the second edition would not have been completed without the encouragement of my wife Alice, our children: Walubita, Nambula, Sipakeli, Nalukui, Siampwila and Mutauka. I also appreciate the encouragement by Bruce Namakando, Rosemary Mwenya Nsunge and the entire Walubita family. Your comments and observations were most useful. I am grateful to my co-author *Woman Power in Politics*, Monde Sifuniso, who never got tired of my constant inquiries.

There were many other people who helped me in one way or another. Your names might not appear here, but my thanks to you are written in my heart. I must thank the Times of Zambia and Zambia Daily Mail for allowing me to use their pictures. Without them, this book would not have seen its second dawn.

After the first dawn of this book, Zambia suffered one of its worst moments in soccer history when the entire national team, officials, Airforce crew, and a journalist died in a plane crash on 28 April 1993 on their way to Senegal for the 1994 World Cup qualifying soccer match. Gone were: players – Richard Mwanza, Moses Masuwa, Winter Mumba, Patrick Banda, Moses Chikwalakwala, Wisdom Chansa, Timothy Mwitwa, Numba Mwila, Derby Mankinka, Godfrey Kangwa, Whiteson Changwe, Eston Mulenga, Samuel Chomba, Kelvin Mutale, Robert Watiyakeni, John Soko, Efford Chabala and Kennan Simambe; officials – Michael Mwape (Chairman of the Football Association of Zambia/delegation leader), Nelson Zimba, Government representative (Ministry of Sport, Youth and Child Development); coaches – Alex Chola, Godfrey Chitalu; team doctor Wilson Mtonga, manager Wilson Sakala; crew – Col. Feston M'hone, Lt. Col. Victor Mubanga, Lt. Col. James Sacika, Flight Engineer Edward Nambote, and news editor Jim Salimu (Zambia News Agency), now Zambia News and Information Services.

INTRODUCTION

Writing any book on the development of sport in Zambia is a laborious task, the multi-disciplinary, nature of sport, entails a varied look at specific sports. Why write a book then? Was the question friends asked when I set out to research and accomplish the dream which has become a reality after four-and half years of despair and frustration, but, above all, hope. I was caught by despair because what you are about to read was almost a non-starter.

Frustration because people one relied upon for vital information either declined at the last and crucial hour or they were too busy or records were with somebody else who was usually unavailable. This resulted in many postponements of deadlines. But in all this I had hope because in any situation there are those few who are ready to help even at a short notice. In them I found inspiration and determination to persevere against all odds.

Many of those well-meaning helpers, I have not mentioned in this book, but I owe them unending gratitude. Their achievements and help are recognized.

It is impossible to write all the successes of Zambian sportsmen, sportswomen and sports associations in the past forty-seven years Independence. This book was initially meant to have been a send-off to the Zambian team to the 1986 Edinburgh Commonwealth Games in Scotland. Zambia and several other countries, however, boycotted the games in protest again Britain's stand on South Africa. An attempt has been made in few pages to illustrate how Zambia has fared in international competitions. But this book is not a '**Who's Who**' in Zambia sport.

In football, professional and amateur boxing, cricket, badminton, squash, golf and bowls among many, Zambia has scored remarkable successes.

Winning is the goal but participation is paramount for a sportsman or sportswoman, Great names in athletics like Yotham Muleya, badminton queens Christine Nyahoda, Theresa Koloko, Louisa Mukangwa (Mrs. Anaene), Acquinata Moya, Catherine Chisala, professional boxing stars like Lottie Mwale, Chisanda Mutti, Charm Chiteule, Julius Luipa, Hugo Chansa, John Sichula, entertained the Zambian spectators with spectacular skills.

In soccer, Zambia's number one game the performances of maestro Samuel 'Zoom' Ndhlovu, Godfrey Chitalu, Bernard Chanda, Henry Kalimukwa, Emment Kapengwe, Freddie Mwila, Peter Kaumba, Kalusha Bwalya, Charles Musonda (both formerly with professionals Cercle Brugge of Belgium), Poni Muyambango, Ridgeway Liwena and the Nkole brothers – Patrick, Abraham, Edward and Godfrey, were dazzling. Amateur boxers Timothy Feruka, Lottie Mwale (before he turned professional), Keith 'Spinks' Mwila, Chisanda Mutti, David Natta, Chris Kapopo, Lucky Mutale, and many others had their share of success. The biggest single achievement was at the 1984 Los Angeles Olympics in the United States where Mwila won the first medal ever by Zambia in the Olympics. In professional boxing Mwale won the African Boxing Union (ABU) and the Commonwealth light heavyweight titles after dethroning Bagayuko Sounkalo of Mali and Canadian Gary Summerhays. Mwale later lost the titles to Joe Lasisi of Nigeria and Leslie Stewart of Trinidad and Tobago.

Mwale was unstoppable and beat many local and international opponents in Lusaka and overseas. I rate Mwale and Patrick Mambwe as two of the greatest boxers Zambia has ever produced. Mwale twice made unsuccessful attempts at the world titles in America, only to lose in fourth rounds against Mathew Saad Muhammad and Mustafa Muhammad.

Golf, a gentleman's game, continues to prosper with more indigenous Zambians taking to the greens since David Phiri broke the racial barriers in the 1960's. The reader is informed of how Phiri meted out instant justice on a white barman at Nchanga who refused to serve him a beer when the barman openly told Phiri he was not a member. Phiri's worst racial incident was at Nkana Golf Club where a non-player grabbed him and told him caddies were not allowed in locker rooms. Of course he was not a caddie.

I have deliberately devoted much space to golf, boxing and athletics because of exciting information I came across. The talents of athletes Yotham Muleya, Beatrice Lungu, Jane Chikambwe, David Lishebo, Boggar Mushanga, Beauty Banda, Jessyman Wishkoti and Audrey Chikani are also highlighted.

Muleya's rare qualities in long distance did Zambia, then a British colony of Northern Rhodesia, proud. He died in a car accident while on a tour of the USA in November 1959.

From the early age, Muleya chased calves, tied them up and later released them. Athletics came to Muleya rather naturally. But, despite international exposure the performance of Zambian athletes in the All-Africa Games,

Commonwealth Games and Olympics can best be described as hits and misses.

Cricketers have excelled on the international scene, as shown by Pravin Desai who captained the East African team to the Mini World Cup tournament which was held in England in 1986. In regional tournament Zambia cricketers have won the annual East and Central African Sir Robert Menzies Trophy several times.

Under the chairmanship of veteran sports administrator, Father Jude McKenna and sponsorship by the Harrington brothers of Senanga and Livingstone, judo continues to attract both the young and old. In 1986, Zambia finished fourth at the All-Africa Championships in Casablanca, Morocco.

It was, in fact, the recognition by the Party and its Government of the achievements by Zambian sportsmen, sportswomen, administrators and associations that President Kenneth David Kaunda honoured the country's sports personalities with the Sportswinners Day at State House in 1985 and 1986.

M.S. Walubita
LUSAKA
10 October, 1986

SOCCER

For reasons buried in the infinite folds of history, football is undeniably the sport which has won the hearts of the entire world's population – almost, anyway. One only has to look at the multitudes that flock to any major soccer event, and how emotionally carried away these disciples get during the course of the game to appreciate the near – narcotic effect of the game. The entertaining nature of the game itself, the team spirit that it engenders and the inspiration that it offers to the beholders and participants alike, has enabled the game to spread and engulf all 'corners' of the world, its drug-like effects turning all who have had the taste of it into irreversible addicts. Whoever invented the game surely deserves note. But, also people have got so 'high' on the soccer mania that very few – if any bother to know his name.

Zambia has been caught in this soccer mania too. The sport has, in fact, grown to be Zambia's foremost game, whose practitioners have been the country's most frequent and consistent flag-bearers at international sporting competitions since the 1960's.

When Zambia was still learning to stand on her own, players like Howard Mwikuta of the then Broken Hill Warriors (now Kabwe Warriors), Emment Kapengwe of Kitwe United and the more durable Freddie Mwila of Rokana United (Nkana Red Devils) had already started juggling the ball in professional soccer in the late 1960's confirming the high speed at which the Zambians have adapted to the game.

A decade, however, had to pass before more Zambian stars could manage to taste the glamour and rigours of professional soccer. Power Dynamos' left-winger Peter Kaumba and striker Alex Chola had a six-month-stint with Africa Sports Club of Cote d'Ivoire (Ivory Coast) in 1984. Contemporaries Kalusha Bwalya and Charles Musonda both from Mufulira Wanderers, had the gates to their fortunes opened through Cercle Brugge Football Club of

Belgium in early and mid 1986 respectively. Lucky Msiska, Stone Nyirenda and Johnstone Bwalya were also signed on by European clubs.

Individual achievements aside, those ten years were some of the sweetest moments for Zambia in as far as the development of soccer is concerned – moments like the Zambia national team's triumph over the then dreaded Congo Kinshasa (now Congo Leopards) on 6 June 1971. It was a glorious moment when the Congo Kinshasa team, was virtually brought to its knees with a 1-2 defeat in the memorable Africa Cup encounter before a delirious Zambian crowd at the Dag Hammarskjold Stadium in Ndola. Narrow as the result may see, its significance and impact on the Zambian soccer fans was immense. Earlier the Zambian team had suffered an aggregate 1-10 defeat at the hands of the same Congolese team. The victory, therefore, seemed to delete, forever, the bitter memory. It was also enough to erase memories of other earlier defeats by Cameroun and Ethiopia.

Though Zambia went on to lose 0-3 in the return match in Kinshasa later, the victory of Zambia in the first leg match lived on.

The year 1971 was also the year that the Zambia national team got its first full-time expatriate coach, Ante Buselic, a Yugoslav. Though with a tottery beginning, Buselic had a new generation of players, among whom were fullbacks Dick Chama and Dickson Makwaza, turned out to be a remarkable combination which scored resounding success in the seasons that followed. Lesotho, Madagascar, Ethiopia, Nigeria and Kenya crashed like ninepins as 'Buselic's babies' powered their way to the finals of the Africa Cup of Nations and the World Cup zonal play-offs in the following two years.

Having found tremendous talent on individual Zambian players, Buselic's professional sense told him that his main job would be to make the players understand that soccer's magic formula was team-work. With that identified and instilled into the players' consciences, Buselic moulded a tremendously talented and well balanced outfit. As it is generally accepted a team with no star is basically a strong all-round team. Buselic's side confirmed this notion. For years to come, the Zambian national team that featured in the 1974 Africa Cup of Nations finals in Cairo will remain the model of competitive soccer outfits in the country if not in Africa.

The famous line-up of Emmanuel Mwape, Edwin Mbaso, Ackim Musenge, Dick Chama, Dickson Makwaza, Boniface Simutowe, Jani Simulambo, Joseph Mapulanga, Simon 'Kaodi' Kaushi, Bernard Chanda, Brighton Sinyangwe, and substitutes Richard Stephenson and Obby Kapita reached the final at the competition at the first try. It was a historical final and a historic feat.

Zambia finished runners-up to the then famed Zaire Leopards after going down 0-2 in a replay. The teams were deadlocked 1-1 at full time and 2-2 after extra time. Brighton Sinyangwe banged in the spectacular equalizer for Zambia only thirty seconds to the final whistle, after Leopards had scored what had seemed to be the winner in the nineteenth minute of extra-time. Sinyangwe's goal took the breath out of the 55,000 spectators at Nasser Stadium in Cairo, Egypt. Due to the time factor, the officials ruled that the match be replayed.

It was in the replay match that Zambia succumbed 0-2 to let the Leopards to be crowned new Africa Champions. The match went into the history books of the Africa Cup of Nations as the greatest Africa Cup final, and the only final to go into extra- time and replay. Zambia was given a standing ovation by the sysmpathetic crowd which included FIFA President Sir Stanely Rous and former World heavyweight boxing champion Muhammad Ali.

After sailing through the preliminary rounds, Zambia took the tournament in Cairo by storm: An incredible 10 – man Zambian team triumphed 1-0 over Cote d'Ivoire, after two-goal hero Simon 'Kaodi' Kaushi was sent off the pitch for retaliation. Then they humbled Uganda by the same margin to meet Egypt in the final match of their Group 'A'.

Having lost 1-3 to Egypt, Zambia were matched against winners in Group 'B' Congo Brazzaville who had beaten Zaire 2-1 in an elimination match in Alexandria. Congo – Brazzaville were the defending champions then. The excitement of the semi-final could have qualified it for the final as the two teams levelled 2-2 to push the game into extra-time. The goals for Zambia came through Stone Chibwe and Bernard Chanda.

The Congolese misfortune was that Chanda had not yet been through with his act. The uncompromising striker bagged in two more goals for Zambia in the extra thirty minutes to put them through to the final against the 'old rival' Zaire, the 3-2 victors of Egypt. The Zambia/Zaire encounter on that March afternoon would have certainly ranked favourite for the prize had there beena 'Most Dramatic Final' award.

A glamorous avalanche of honours befell the unsuspecting Zambian squad after the splendid performance. Goalkeeper Emmanuel Mwape was voted the best in Africa. Fullback Dick Chama was picked for the All-Africa XI as was striker Bernard Chanda.

such was the quality of the team, that in the wings, Zambia had the best wingers to ever kick the ball in Brighton Sinyangwe and Moses Simwala. Although two players of the younger generation, Peter Kaumba and Kalusha Bwalya, later managed to somewhat dim the memory, Simwala's authority on the right wing still lingers on in the minds of local soccer fans.

Although Kabwe Warriors' Godfrey 'Ucar' Chitalu, Zambia's goalking, had scored a massive 107 goals in the 1972 season – surpassed only by Pele's record 121 netted in 1961 – he was never really a regular with Buselic's team during his five-year-stint.

National soccer slumbered after reaching its peak in 1974. Zambia was eliminated in the preliminaries of the 1974 and 1975 East and Central African Challenge Cup. The story was the same at club level where Green Buffaloes were repeatedly ousted from the African Club Championships Cup from 1974-1976. There was a little stir of life – though not so much – in the national soccer team in 1976 after Buselic's contract had been extended for a year. Even with the absence of some stars of the 1974 Africa Cup squad, Zambia qualified for the Olympic Games Soccer Competition in Montreal, Canada. But the games were marred by the Afro-Arab led political boycott in protest against the presence in Montreal of New Zealand which was the ally of South Africa.

The soccer team later returned home, having played only one game and lost 2-3 to Canada. That was the first and, to date, the only time that Zambia played against a North American team.

The North American experience seemed to have restored the national team's ebbed morale and added some impetus to its run for international recognition through zonal and regional competitions. Starting from late 1976, Zambia reached the final of the eight-nation ECA Challenge Cup competition three times in three consecutive years. Magnificent as the run was, the end was consistently inconclusive. Zambia succumbed 0-2 to Uganda Cranes in Zanzibar in 1976, fate was in favour of the Cranes the following year again as Zambia bowed out of the final with a 4-5 defeat on penalties, and crumbled 3-2 at the hands of their own apprentices, Malawi in 1978. The defeat by Malawi was the one that hurt the Zambians most. Only two years previously, Zambia had virtually been teaching the Malawian team how to play soccer. In friendly games, Zambia could score as many goals as the players felt. But then to see the trophy which the 'teachers' had been burning their lungs out to own for so long casually slip into the hands of a team which they had nurtured themselves; and to think that the novices had beaten the 'teachers' in the last fight for the treasure, was very unbearable indeed.

It was these ominous experiences – especially the last two against Uganda and Malawi – which made the country's soccer fans believe that the Zambian national team was cursed with perpetual bad luck a belief which has not yet been completely abandoned by some staunch disciples of superstition. Who could blame them anyway with the power that the game has to excite the emotional reserves of its revelers? What with the fact that earlier in the same year, Zambia was eliminated in the preliminary rounds of the Africa Cup of Nations finals staged in Accra, Ghana, in what was supposed to be a dramatic come-back after being absent for three years since the 1974 storm.

Zambia lost 1-2 to hosts Ghana's Black Stars. Obby Kapita scored the only goal for Zambia after a cross from Godfrey Chitalu. The new-look line-up comprised Vincent Chileshe, Bernard Mutale, Kaiser Kalambo, Robert Lutoba, Ackim Musenge, Evans Katebe, Moses Simwala, Jani Simulambo, Alex Chola, Chitalu and Kapita.

The second game was a consolation 2-0 victory over Upper Volta (now Burkina Faso). Patrick Phiri and second-half substitute Bizwell Phiri shared one goal a piece in each half in the face – saver. Willie Phiri, another formidable, hard-running linkman also joined the game in the second-half.

In the final preliminary tie in Group 'A', Zambia fought to a painful goalless draw against Nigeria in what was the toughest class to be played in the 1978 finals. Displaying superiority in ball-control and distribution, it could only be 'bad luck' that the game could not go in Zambia's favour. As it was, the draw – consigned the Zambian team out of the race. The team, captained by Ackim Musenge, returned home to start afresh, hoping to do better next time.

The next time would be two years later but instead of the Africa Nations Cup, the occasion this time was the 1980 Olympic Games in Moscow, USSR. Zambia went to Soviet Union in place of Egypt who had joined the United States' led boycott of the games.

The performance, however, could have been better. Zambia lost 1-0 to Cuba, in their opening match, sank 3 – 1 to the Soviet Union after levelling 1 – 1 at half-time, and went down 2-1 to Venezuela with the winning goal coming only thirty seconds before full-time. The experience was unique to the Zambian team in that it was a rare chance of being exposed to exotic and polished play.

In pursuit of the lost glory, and wanting to repeat the 1974 feat, Zambia staged a storming return to the African Nations Cup in 1982 in Libya. In one of the most exciting African Cup finals to be ever staged, Zambia finished third in the competition after beating Algeria 2-0 in the third and fourth place play-off in Tripoli.

Zambia went down 1-2 to hosts Libya in the semi-finals. Zambia had defeated Ethiopia 1-0 and routed Nigeria 3-0 to finish runners-up to Algeria who had earlier beaten them 1-0 in the Group 'B' opening match in Benghazi.

Enjoying massive home support, Libya scored the winning goal eight minutes to full-time through a free-kick in the penalty box. The two teams had tied 1-1 at half-time. Tough and bruising would be the most fitting description of the play throughout the Zambia/Libya match.

Though Zambia did not reach the final this time, the performance would actually be the best up to then considering that the tournament was being played at a time when football standards had improved tremendously throughout Africa. It was everybody's feeling that the time had now come for Zambia to win a Cup, after observing the skill and game control which the team displayed during the course of the event. But as the then Football Association of Zambia (FAZ) chairman, Tom Mtine, said 'God had not decided yet for Zambia to win the Cup.'

The national team, however, consoled itself by winning the two – nation Confederation of African Football (CAF) Jubilee tournament in Cairo in 1982. And, although it just passed unsung, another honour was brought to the nation when the Under 20 national team won the inaugural Confederation of Southern African Football Association's Cup in 1983.

A shock 2-1 first round aggregate defeat by Sudan shattered hopes of Zambia appearing at the 1984 final in Cote d'Ivoire (Ivory Coast).

In the second leg game played at Dag Hammarskjold Stadium in Ndola, Alex Chola, who scored the only goal in Khartoum's first leg match, missed a decisive penalty for Zambia following a foul on Peter Kaumba by El Ismail in the penalty box. Zairean referee Mpundu Chisalaba, awarded Zambia the penalty, but to the amazement of the capacity home crowd, Chola's shot was parried away by Sudanese goalkeeper Hamid Berima.

The defeat, however, served Zambia well as it made them decide to re-enter the East and Central African Cup Competition in Uganda, after staying away for three successive years. This decision was to be the one which would forever be renewed by the Zambian soccer fraternity. Whether it was an instinctive move, or a calculated one is immaterial. The fact is that it was the beginning of the sweetest soccer experience that Zambia would ever have at least to-date.

Well aware of the odds against them Zambia boldly marched ahead to test their might against Zimbabwe, Tanzania, Kenya, Malawi, Somalia, Zanzibar and hosts Uganda in Kampala. Kenya's Harambee Stars were defending the Cup after grabbing it from Malawi the previous year. Like Malawi, Kenya had a consolidated team, the players having been retained for a number of years. Zimbabwe were the upstarts in the competition, only four years old after attaining national independence in April 1980. However, they had grown so fast in terms of football that they were almost on par with Zambia, a team twenty years old.

Goalkeepers Efford Chabala, Ghost Mulenga and Vincent Chileshe; defenders Jones Chilengi (captain), Fighton Simukonda, Ben Pabili, Kapambwe Mulenga, Laban Chishala, Thomas Mwale and Mustafa Kalizamani; midfielders Bright Mangambwa, Dominic Mutale Jericho Shinde and Willie Chibwika; forwards Lucky Msiska, Bonnie Muma, John Zyambo, Fanny Hangunyu, Harrison Bwalya, Jack Chanda and Kalusha Bwalya made up the full team which travelled to Uganda. They were led by the first fulltime local coach, Colonel Brightwell Banda, and team doctor Patrick Ngosa.

At a psychological advantage considering that the other teams regarded Zambia's presence as the strongest threat, the Zambian squad first pushed aside Zimbabwe with a 2-0 send-off in their opening Group 'A' match at Nakivubo Stadium in Kampala. The match sent warning shots to their Group 'A' teams Tanzania and Uganda who could not escape confrontation with Zambia. The standard of play displayed in the match was such that a Zambian soccer official, Winson Gumboh, said he had never seen the national team play so well in many years.

Although the victory over Zimbabwe was a psychological booster for the next preliminary clash against Taifa Stars of Tanzania, Zambia could not just storm into the field, bulging with premature confidence. The encounter with Tanzania needed not to be approached with timidity as the Taifa Stars had caused Zambia a lot of misery on previous occasions. In 1980, the imponderable Stars had wreaked havoc on Zambia in the preliminaries of the Africa Cup of Nations competition. After losing 0-1 in Dar-es-Salaam, Zambia were held to a 1-1 draw with a home- support advantage. The Stars were to repeat the feat the following year when they laid Zambia prone on the turf with 2-1 blasting in the semi-finals of the championships.

It was with this background that Zambia entered the pitch with their teeth clenched, and their jaws firm with confidence. They just managed to extinguish the cunning Stars with a 2-1 beating. It was hurrah for Zambia nonetheless for the victory got them an obvious semi-final berth. With the situation at two down one to go, Zambia approached the Group 'A' top slot and second place play-off against Uganda with relative relaxation. They had nothing to lose anyway. They needed to reserve as much energy as they could for the semi-final clash.

Having won both their first two matches, Zambia was leading the group with four points. Uganda had three points from one win and a draw while Zimbabwe and Tanzania had not won a single match. Therefore even if Zambia were to lose against Uganda, she would still be one of the top two in the group, tying four points each with Uganda. But then Uganda had a better goal difference, so, tying on points meant Zambia a dangerous situation in which she would be drawn against the winners of Group 'B' in the semi-finals. To ensure that she had a more favourable semi-final clash, Zambia had to maintain the top slot and finish as the winner of Group 'A' but at the same time, attain this without expending too much of her reserves.

So then, for the seemingly invincible Zambians, the game against Uganda was purely of academic importance. What with the fact that the Uganda Cranes were supposed to have brought in some new faces after earlier defeats by Zambia in the World Cup series and Tanzania in the Africa Cup of Nations. Even though Zambia had eliminated the Cranes on goal – aggregate, the last victory had gone to Uganda the previous August when they slapped Zambia 1-0 in the first round, second leg match. Both teams had to be cautious without being too timid.

A second minute goal by hard-running Jack Chanda was disallowed. But it was later to be recovered through a spot-kick converted by skipper Jones Chilengi.

An equalizer for the Cranes was hotly disputed by Zambian players and officials who thought it was an off-side but in vain. The referee's decision was final. With this 1-1 deadlock, the game ended, and it was as good as a victory for Zambia. They remained on top of their group and were to negotiate the second placed Group 'B' team – Kenya in the semi-finals.

Harambee Stars of Kenya were no strangers to the Zambians neither were they easy meat. From 1964 to the time the 1984 East and Central African Senior Challenge Cup competition was taking place, the two national teams had clashed a record thirty-one times. Both had won fourteen times each and they had drawn three times. Fifty – fifty! But Zambia had a slight daunting edge over the Kenyans. In the 1978 ECA competition in Lilongwe, Malawi, Zambia had stamped an indelible mark on the Kenyans and the coach fired.

'The Bombers,' as the Zambian team had come to be called by supporters in Kampala, could not be said to have been in their maximum state of composure when they entered the pitch. Even with the clear no-loss record backing them up in the competition, the Harambee Stars gave their first real tough match. Although they had finished second after Malawi in their Group 'B' matches, the stars were playing to show that they had it in their blood to fight when they wanted. After all, they were the defending champions.

At full time the scoreboard was as blank as when the first whistle was blown, and the match dragged into extra-time. But, alas, fate deceived the Kenyans as they found it impossible to hold back the surging Philemon Mulala of Zambia. Twice Mulala sought the Kenyans' net in either half of extra-time, and twice, he shook it. There was no response from Kenya, and the final whistle found them still in a state of shock.

The score-board screamed 2-0 for Zambia as 'The Bombers' made their jubilant exit from Nakivubo Stadium, basking in the deafening roar of away support. The support which shamed the soccer fans at home as they held their transistor radios tightly to their ears, trying to catch the word from the 'swallowed up' voice of soccer commentator Denis Liwewe.

Zambia had - AGAIN – qualified for the final of the East and Central

Africa Senior Challenge Cup competition. Zambia was to meet Malawi, who had wrapped up Uganda 2-0 in their semi-final encounter.

Seeing that the team had gone that far in isolation, the Zambian public was suddenly jacked upright from its slouched and arrogant posture. It realized that the team needed reassurance from home at such a crucial point. A touch of home would surely serve the team well in inspiring confidence and maintaining the composure. Though the Kampala crowd was in favour of Zambia, in that Malawi had evicted their own team, the backing lacked personal touch, that familiar nudge and affinity.

Zambia Airways put up a chartered plane to fly fans to Kampala for the final match. Mr. Rupiah Bwezani Banda was appointed to organize the flight. Currently, His Excellency The President of the Republic of Zambia.

He was assisted by Bank of Zambia general Manager, Michael Mwape and Grandson Ngoma, a prominent businessman from Chipata to organize a total of 160 fans which Zambia Airways needed to release the plane. Each one of them was required to pay K873.00 for the trip.

Would it help at all? may have been the question spinning through every Zambian soccer fan's mind as the Zambia/Malawi final match dragged on and on goalless. First half, second half – nothing. Extra time!

Transistor radios became a treasure on that December afternoon. Here and there, a tight group of transfixed fans gave all their ears to the radio commentary all over Zambian townships. Nobody shifted an inch in case he misses out on any important moment – even at break. The crowds grew quieter as the extra time seemingly 'flew' to the last minutes, expectantly bending towards the radio every time the commentator's voice rose a fraction of a note higher. And then it was over. No change. Still nothing!

Soccer's most dreaded moment came when it was ruled that the final would end in a penalty shoot-out. Zambia scored their first two shots.

But it was goalkeeper Efford Chabala who turned the tables for Zambia. Chabala saved Malawi's first two shots while Zambia scored another one to make it 3-0. Malawi resigned, and that was how Zambia hauled the first major silverware after years of fervent pursuit.

The local fans were joyous lot savering the glorious moment. Nothing else seemed to matter.

Prime Minister Nalumino Mundia, led a host of top state officials, sports administrators, and hundreds of soccer fans who received the gallant squad at Lusaka's International Airport. On that afternoon, 17 December 1984 there was a light drizzle, but the jubilant throng could not be put off.

Team captain Jones Chilengi, descended from the Zambian Airways Boeing 707 aircraft, bearing the East and Central Africa Senior Challenge Cup in his hands

Chilengi was voted the best sweeper in the competition while Kalusha Bwalya was voted best left-winger and Philemon Mulala best right-winger. But the hero of the final was, undisputably, twenty-four year old goalkeeper, Efford Chabala. He was hoisted shoulder high by fans at the airport. President Milton Obote, had feted Zambian supporters at the State House in Entebbe. Team coach Brightwell Banda was promoted to full Colonel by then President Kenneth D, Kaunda as Commander-in-Chief of the Zambia Defence Forces.

With the regional mission accomplished with such resounding success and finesse Zambia set her sights higher with the turn of the year. Having gathered confidence with the lifting of the ECA Challenge Cup, she would now have a full-speed go at the continental cup being staged in March 1986. But before that there was still 1985 to be negotiated with its World Cup Africa Zone qualifying rounds against Cameroun in April and the inevitable defence of the ECA Challenge Cup later in October.

The 'Indomitable Lions' of Cameroun roared into Lusaka on April 4 determined not to settle for anything less than the complete annihilation of the flamboyant Zambian side in the second round; first leg confrontation at Lusaka's Independence Stadium. The city shook with terror and nail-biting anxiety as the Lions invaded the local soccer scene with menacing calmness. Not a single word of bragging could be solicited from the Camerounian camp as the day drew closer, but their threatening presence was enough to make local soccer fans abandon their seats for a while as they fought hard to brush off their nervousness and maintain the cool.

Continuously, the fans filtered into the stadium on April 7 the day of the clash. The gates were opened as early as 08.00hours in anticipation of the largest turn-out ever. True, the turn-out was such that the Football Association of Zambia (FAZ) registered a record K199, 997 in gate takings. Everybody wanted to see the 'Indomitable Lions', a name the Camerounians acquired when they lifted the African Cup of Nations in 1984. The Zambian massacre was too obvious and the fans wanted to be there so they could see for themselves how their team would be torn into pieces. Since the sealing of the marriage bond in December 1984 when the team brought them regional glory, it was 'till death doth us part' with the Zambian fans.

When the game kicked off at last, the fans who seemed to have occupied the stadium to the last centimeter including a capacity crowd perched outside, on the Humanism Hill, fell into such a silence that one could have thought it was a funeral gathering. The moment of truth had come, and there could not be any wild cheering without prior analysis. Timidity had to be exercised.

But the fans were shocked out of all fear when the elusive Zambian frontliners whizzed past the yawning Lions with a fast four-goal blast up their throats in the first half. Courageous centre-forward Jack Chanda was the man of the match as he kept the Camerounian defence on its heels, in full flight after his hard – going physique, making accurate passes to left-winger Kalusha Bwalya and striker Michael Chabala.

The fans were continuously on their feet in a pleasurable frenzy screaming Zambia! Zambia! As Michael Chabala broke the ice in the first half of twenty-one minutes, Aaron Njovu quickly followed it up with another beauty three minutes later. Having identified the Lions' soft spot, it only took another three minutes for Chabala to place the ball past the Camerounian goalkeeper for Zambia's third goal.

Utilising Chanda's intelligent moves to the full, it was Chabala again who shook the Camerounian net in the thirty-second minute only five minutes after his last goal. A hat-trick for Chabala, and 4-0 for Zambia was the situation at half time. Independence Stadium was a hive of 'possessed' human beings that April afternoon.

In the second half, Zambia played entertaining soccer, for they had got whatever there was to get in the first half. A fumble in the seventy-fourth minute gave the 'tamed' Lions a chance to score their face-saver. The final whistle blew with the situation still standing at 4-1 for Zambia.

Colonel Brightwell Banda's line-up that afternoon had been Efford Chabala, Fighton Simukonda, Kapambwe Mulenga, John Mwanza, Jones Chilengi, Jericho Shinde, Phillimon Mulala (Lucky Msiska), Aaron Njovu (Derby Mankinka), Michael Chabala, Jack Chanda and Kalusha Bwalya.

Among the thousands of fans who watched the thrilling performance by the Zambian team that afternoon, was His Excellency Dr. Kenneth David Kaunda, then President of the Republic of Zambia.

During the preparations for the clash, the Zambian team had been given maximum attention by the public. When the team was camped, Chief Mpezeni of the Ngoni in the Eastern Province had donated a whole cow to feed the players during camp. The Cold Storage Corporation had also donated beef. Zambia Electricity Supply Corporation (ZESCO) had presented the team with five brand new Yugoslav-made Europa balls for use during training. For this reason, the team's victory was also the victory of the general public.

Camerounian team coach, Rade Ognanovic, pledged that he would spend sleepless nights to find a suitable formula to subdue Zambia in the return leg, in Yaounde, Cameroun, on April 21. But Zambia would not just sit idle. Knowing that tables could turn in Yaoundé with a swamping home support for the Lions, FAZ was prepared to spend K100,000 if only to fly 115 supporters to Cameroun on a Zambian Airways Boeing 737.

Cameroun recalled their four professional players, from Europe for the second leg match, demonstrating the seriousness with which they took the match. It was their decisive moment if they were to remain in the race for the World Cup place. Goalkeeper Thomas Nkono and left-winger Rodger Milla were flown from European clubs – Barcelona and St. Etiene respectively to come and feature in their national team.

Before a Camerounian crowd in Yaounde, plus the token Zambian supporters, the two teams lay side by side in a 1-1 stalemate after a gruelling fight. Jones Chilengi scored for Zambia. The Zambian team returned home to a hero's welcome.

While in Cameroun, skipper Jones Chilengi, Jack Chanda and Michael Chabala were approached by two top French clubs to play professional soccer.

First division Rennes Football Club hunted Chilengi and Chanda while Michael Chabala was approached by a team called Dynamos. Even national team coach Col. Banda had his share of advances from foreign countries which wanted to recruit him.

In the third round draws, Zambia were billed against Algeria. Zambia went down hard when Algeria gave them a 2-0 blast in Algeria. That was to mark the beginning of the end of Zambia's courageous race for world honours.

The faithful home crowd filled the Independence Stadium in Lusaka, Zambia, to an all-time record capacity in the return leg encounter in July. As goodwill always overcomes bad, the defeat in Algeria could never erase the 4-1 victory over Cameroun earlier in the year. Like they had done with the Camerounian clash, Zambian fans would die together with their team. And, indeed, they died in unity as the fast-running Algerians scored the only goal in the match to lead 3-0 on aggregate. That was the thrashing which Zambia got for being so cunning. No more World Cup hopes. At least for a long time while the Algerians flew away with the victory, the Football Association of Zambia was counting its lucky stars. The match had netted in a record – breaking K323, 490 from gate-takings, the greatest amount collected in the history of Zambian football. Go ye Algerians with our blessing, as your victory brings us fortune.

With the World Cup hopes dashed in this manner, what remained for Zambia was just to revive their long-lost prestige in the continental competition. Immediately the Algerians flew off, the Zambian team flew after them, but headed to Nigeria, where they were to meet the Green Eagles in the first leg of the final African Cup of Nations qualifying round. Zambia had gone through to the final round without a drop of sweat after Ethiopia withdrew from the tournament. Nigeria, who had also qualified in a similar way after Tanzania withdrew, were Zambia's last hurdle to the finals. The two teams had last met in the 1982 finals when Zambia triumphed 3-0 to reach the semi-finals.

There were no scores at all in the first leg match in Lagos. When the Eagles landed at the International Airport in Lusaka for the second leg battle it was no jokes right from the beginning. The Zambian soccer officials and journalists received the shock of their careers when they beheld the amount of luggage that was tugged along by the Nigerian team. The Eagles had brought along their own food, a portable stove and their own cook. No Zambian food was going to be eaten by the powerful Eagles in case it was contaminated. Neither would they risk having a strange cook prepare their food, let along prepare it in strange utensils. Everything would be kept as Nigerian as possible to make the Eagles feel at home and not lose confidence.

But all this was a sheer waste of energy and money. The Eagles were deplumed with narrow 1-0 shave by Zambia. Jack Chanda made the noble copper eagle on the Zambian flag fly higher than the Green Eagles from Nigeria with an eighty-sixth goal. The noble eagle was on its way to Cairo, Egypt, for the 1986 African Cup of Nations finals, proud and free.

Shelving the African Cup mission for a while, Zambia flew to Zimbabwe in October 1985 to defend, the East and Central African Senior Challenge Cup which they lifted in 1984.

With the complacency of being the defending champions, and puffed up with the recent victory over Nigeria, Zambia was too confident to compete with Tanzania, Kenya, Uganda, Zimbabwe and Malawi. In their first Group 'B' match, Zambia were drawn against Malawi, the 1984 losing finalists. Obviously Malawi were out to avenge the 0-3 defeat of the previous year and, as Zambia coach, Colonel Brightwell Banda said, because of traditional rivalry the Malawians viewed victory over Zambia as 'better than winning the World Cup.'

At Barbourfields Stadium in Bulawayo, Zambia and Malawi drew 2-2. Zambia took longer to settle and Malawi scored the first goal in the thirteenth minute. When Jack Chanda equalized in the twenty-nineth minute, the Malawians came to lead again twenty-two minutes into second half. The equalizer was scored by Ben Pabili (now Bamfuchile), a few minutes to full-time. Banda attributed the results to the erratic defence system.

Fielding Efford Chabala, Laban Chishala, Mustafa Kalizamani, Ben Pabili, Jones Chilengi, Alex Chola, Jericho Shinde, Jack Chanda, Chilufya Mwenya, Stone Nyirenda, Michael Chabala and Kalusha Bwalya, the conceited Zambia slumped 0-3 to Uganda in their second Group 'B' match. The Zambians had been so certain that they would pull through the crucial match and increase their chances of retaining the cup before the game. As it was with only six teams competing the defeat automatically ejected them from the competition as they lagged at the bottom of the Group. Thus, Zambia gave away the East and Central Africa Senior Challenge Cup, the only glimmer in Zambia's soccer history.

Zimbabwe won the cup after beating Kenya 2-0 in the final.

The Zambia national team, empty-handed returned to the coldest reception in a long time. The atmosphere tense, the players found not a single soul to receive them at the airport. Even the airport workers acted as if they did not recognize the national team. The players showed themselves into the VIP lounge, and for the first time, the players and officials were made to pay customs duty on items bought in Botswana and Zimbabwe.

Even with the team's performance in Zimbabwe, the Zambia Coaches Association led by Samuel 'Zoom' Ndhlovu still backed Colonel Brightwell Banda's selection of the team. However, a suggestion came up that the coach be sent to Europe for a refresher course in preparation for the African Cup of Nations the following March in Egypt.

Against this backdrop, Zambia realized that if she were to do a good job in the 1986 continental Cup finals, she should start early and leave no stone unturned in her preparations. A chance four-nation Zairean invitation in November 1985 was indeed received by Zambia as manna from heaven. Zambia would clash against resurgent Zaire Leopards, Egypt and Ivory Coast (Cote d'Ivoire) at the May 25 Stadium in Kinshasa. FAZ did not waste time to put up K45, 000 to camp the national team for ten days.

Four ex-internationals were called back to the national team by the FAZ technical committee formed in October 1985, comprising the former second Vice-Chairman Mr. Rupiah Bwezani Banda (currently His Excellency the President of the Republic of Zambia), treasurer Barney Bungoni, Lackson Kazabu, Abram Mokola, Samuel 'Zoom' Ndhlovu and Colonel Brightwell Banda.

Recalled were the towering sweeper Fighton Simukonda, fullback Thomas Mwale, forward Boyd Chilembo and winger Philemon Mulala. These filled in the spaces left by Alex Chola, John Mwanza and Vincent Chileshe who were dropped. Other inclusions were Charles Musonda, Ignatius Muswala, Peter Mwanza, Webby Chilufya, Edwin Kanyanta, Happy Simfukwe, Harrison Simwala and Joseph Ngoma.

The team later lost to Egypt in the final match of the four-nation tournament which took place from November 19 – 24.

In February 1986, only a month before the finals in Egypt, Zambia played four friendlies as three countries as part of her intensive preparatory programme. Zambia beat Botswana 9-0 on aggregate in two friendlies played in Ndola and Lusaka. Later Zambia survived defeat to draw 2-2 against Malawi in Lusaka. Malawi led 2-1 at half time.

Zambia was invited to Saudi Arabia to play some friendlies during a ten-day all expenses – paid for stay in transit to Egypt. With the hope that the Saudi Arabian stay would help the players acclimatize to the Saudi weather which was similar to that of Egypt, coach Brightwell Brightwell Banda, assisted by Boniface Simutowe, and technical advisor Samuel 'Zoom' Ndhlovu flew with the team. During their stay, Zambia lost 0-1 to the Saudi national team through a penalty in the eightieth minute. A correspondent in Saudi Arabia, attributed the defeat to fatigue. The game was played within five hours of Zambia's arrival in Saudi Arabia, after two sleepless nights. The team played two more games against top clubs winning one by a 2-1 margin and drawing the other 1-1.

By then, Kalusha Bwalya had already been signed on by Cercle Brugge of Belgium and he would join the team in Egypt straight from Belgium.

The twenty-man squad included four survivors from the 1982 finals in Libya. These were midfielder/defender Ashios Melu, midfielder Jericho Shinde, striker Jack Chanda and defender Jones Chilengi. The new inclusions were Langson Phiri, Boniface Chanda, Charles Musonda, Chilufya Mwenya and Webby Chilufya.

The full squad was goalkeepers: Efford Chabala and Peter Banda; defenders Laban Chishala, Peter Mwanza, Kapambwe Mulenga, Jones Chilengi, Webby Chilufya, Ashios Melu and Edwin Kanyanta; midfielders Charles Musonda, Derby Mankinka, Langson Phiri and Jericho Shinde; strikers: Jack Chanda, Chilufya Mwenya, Boniface Chanda, Michael Chabala, Hector Chisompola, Wisdom Chansa and Kalusha Bwalya.

After the 5-2 aggregate victory of the previous year, Zambia played very confidently in the opening Group 'B' match against Cameroun. But the hard-fighting and determined Zambia were cut to size by the not so hungry looking Lions with 2-3 defeat in a badly handled match. Trailing 0-1 through a forty-seventh minute goal by professional Rodger Milla, Zambia were denied two clear penalties in the first half by a Malian referee. Zambia equalized through an awesome header in the sixty-third minute by Michael Chabala. Chabala still gave the Camerounian defenders a headache.

Cameroun were awarded a penalty three minutes later which Louis Paul M'fede converted to lead 2-1, but another penalty awarded to Zambia fifteen minutes later put the teams on the level again. But the referee was not through with his penalty galore yet as Kalusha Bwalya's equalizer was nullified by another penalty awarded to Cameroun a few minutes later. 3-2 for Cameroun was the final score.

Having won the hearts of the North African fans through their captivating style of play, the Zambians received an overwhelming call to purported unfairness. The Egyptian fans felt that Zambia was the better of the two teams and she was just robbed of her victory. Letters from Egypt and phone calls reached the local press, calling on Zambia to pull out of the finals as she was never going to reach anywhere with the kind of bias abound in Egypt.

Playing excellent soccer, Zambia held a star-studded Algerian side to a 0-0 draw in the second match. Algeria had eight professionals playing in the match and it was as much as Zambia could do to draw with them. Being so crucial, however, it was the most heart-breaking result which Zambian soccer fans could expect. A win at this point would have strengthened Zambia's position in the group, and a possible semi-final berth. It was at this point that Col. Banda was quoted as saying resignedly, 'In both our matches, we have fought very hard taking the ball to our enemy. But luck has not been with us.'

The third game against Morocco made things even worse. Though fighting as hard as in the first two matches, Zambia were pipped 0-1 by the fast running Moroccans. That was the end of the race.

The boys put in as much as they could but they had been unlucky to have lost in their first game. The draw against the Algerians was not too bad at all, considering that they beat Zambia only a few months previously and they would represent Africa at the World Cup finals in Mexico. Besides, it was an all round professional side. Zambia only had one professional, Kalusha Bwalya, who had been in Belgium for only a few months. Morocco were obviously a tough side. They were also to represent Africa in Mexico with Algeria.

Such has been the rough and smooth path Zambian soccer has traversed since attaining Independence in 1964. The period covered though not wholly representative, at least outlines the typical Zambia soccer scene at national level. Club soccer, has progressed well over the same period.

Kabwe Warriors made Zambia's debut in the African Champion Clubs Cup in 1972. The Railway men were drawn against Ghana's legendary Accra Hearts of Oak and produced a sensational result. A downpour shortly after the match had started turned the pitch into a quagmire. Warriors leading 2-0 before the break were literally caught with the wrong books on. Handicapped, Warriors crashed 2-7 to Hearts and in the return leg in Lusaka; they were spiritless as they lost 1-2.

Warriors, who had won all the domestic cups in 1972 represented Zambia again in 1973 but were again tossed out in the first round by Asante Kotoko also from Ghana, on 3-2 aggregate.

From 1974-76, Green Buffaloes carried the Zambian banner in the Champion Clubs Cup, with no success.

Mufulira Wanderers, who had brought the Castle Cup (now Independence Cup) into Zambia after beating City Wanderers of Southern Rhodesia

(Zimbabwe) 4-3, were the nation's hopes in 1977. They reached the semi-finals, but Accra Hearts of Oak again curtailed the Zambian challenge. Wanderers had won 5-2 in Lusaka but went out on the away-goals-count-double rule after losing 0-3 in Ghana.

In 1978, Wanderers took part in the African Cup Winners' Cup for the second time. Three years previously, they had automatically qualified to the semi-finals of the inaugural tournament. The reached the semi-finals again in 1978, but Algeria's Mahd Soccer Club halted their progress, once again on the away-goals-count-double rule. Wanderers had triumphed 2-1 in Lusaka but sank 0-1 in Algiers.

The only exception at the club level was 1982 when Power Dynamos went all the way in the Cup Winners' Cup. They met Egypt's Arab Contractors in the two-legged final. But, alas, success eluded Zambia as Dynamos lost 0-2, 0-2 away and at home.

Despite these drawbacks at international level, the domestic scene has not been without its memorable occasions. In 1972 for instance, Kabwe Warriors, then boasting of the best players in the country swept all the honours. Fielding stars like Richard Stephenson, Godfrey 'Ucar' Chitalu, Sandy Kaposa, Peter Nyongani, Gibby Zulu, Sandford Mvula, the cunning midfield tactician Boniface Simutowe and defender Edward Musonda, won the Castle Cup, Chibuku Cup, Shell and BP Challenge Cup and the league Championship.

Wanderers, the club which hit the headlines in 1978, nearly emulated the feat that year. With the likes of national team skipper Ackim Musenge, Abraham Nkole, Patrick Nkole, Edward Nkole, Daniel Mutale, Thomas Bwalya, Evans Katebe, Benson 'Swift' Musonda, and Robertson Zulu, at their peak, Wanderers reached the finals of all major Cups. But history was not to be repeated.

Wanderers lost 2-3 to Buffaloes in the renamed Chibuku Cup, 2-3 again to Roan United in the Challenge Cup, but at last managed to edge Red Arrows 2-1 and lift the Castle Cup (renamed Independence Cup). Mighty Wanderers also retained the league championship.

But the tendency has changed as the years advance. It is becoming very rare indeed to find that one team wins more than two cups, not even retain the league championship for two successive years. The tendency in the past was such that very few firms sponsored football clubs. Therefore, players rushed to the sponsored clubs, making them the strongest teams. But as more firms have got interested in the game, more talented players have developed within their own areas, making more strong teams and rendering competition stiff.

Nkana Red Devils (formerly Rokana United) had tried to maintain formidability for a number of years. Maybe owing to the fact that most of the players in the team are superbly built in physique. But Mufulira Wanderers remained the team which produced the most stars to-date. Charles Musonda was the international from the club who joined Kalusha Bwalya, a team-mate, in Belgium for a four-year professional stint. The two were not the first professionals from Zambia and they surely will not be the last as soccer continues to improve in Zambia.

SUMMARY OF SOME MAJOR SOCCER RESULTS

MARCH 1981

(Africa Cup Winners' Cup – Kitwe)
Power Dynamos 2 Matlama (Lesotho) 0
The two sides earlier drew 1-1

APRIL

(International Friendlies)
Zambia 4 Congo1, Zambia 1 Congo 1

(World Cup first leg second round in Harare)
Zambia 1, Zimbabwe 0

(Zone Six Tournament)
Zambia B 6 Swaziland 1, Zambia 2 Zimbabwe 0

MAY

Africa Cup Winners' Cup second round, first leg)
Power Dynamos 1 Palmeiras Beira (Mozambique) 1
(Second leg)
Dynamos 5, Palmeiras Beira 0

(Africa Cup of Champion Club second round, first leg in Maputo)
Nchanga Rangers 3, Desportes de Sol (Mozambique) 1
(Second leg)
Rangers 3, Desportes 1

JUNE

(International Friendlies)
Zambia 3, Zaire Leopards 1 (Chingola).
Zambia 3, Zaire 3 (Lusaka)

SEPTEMBER

Africa Cup of Champion Clubs (Kinshasa)
Nchanga Rangers 1 Vita (Zaire) 4 Second leg: Rangers 2, Vita 0
(Chingola).

The match ended prematurely after the Ugandan referee Bukenge
walked off the pitch, four minutes to full time.
Africa Cup Winners' Cup – Quarter-Finals: Secondi Hassacas (Ghana) 3
Power Dynamos 1, Power Dynamos 1 Hassacas 0

MARCH 1982

(Africa Cup of Nations finals, Libya)
Zambia 0 Algeria 1
Zambia 1 Ethiopia 0
Zambia 3 Nigeria 0

(Semi-Finals)
Zambia 1 Libya 2

Third and Fourth Place play-offs
Zambia 2 Algeria 0

(Africa Cup Winners' Cup first round, first leg. Jinja)
Power Dynamos 0, Uganda Coffee 0

Second Leg:
Dynamos 2 Uganda Coffee 0

African Cup of Champion Clubs second round, first leg (Lusaka)
Green Buffaloes 0, Vital'o (Burundi) 0

Second Leg:
Buffaloes 2 Vital'o 0

MAY

(Africa Cup Winners' second round, first leg – Arusha)
Power Dynamos 0, Pan African (Tanzania) 1

Return Leg:
Dynamos 5, Pan African 3

(African Cup of Champions Clubs Third Round, first leg – Lusaka) Green
Buffaloes 3 A.S. Somasud (Madagascar) 0.

Return Leg:
Buffaloes 3 A.S. Somasud 1

SEPTEMBER

(Africa Cup Winners' Cup quarter finals first leg – Harare)
Power Dynamos 2, Caps United (Zimbabwe) 1

Return Leg:
Power Dynamos 3 Caps 0

(Africa Cup of Champion Clubs quarter finals first leg – Cairo)
Green Buffaloes 1, National (Egypt) 3

Return Leg:
Buffaloes 1, National 0

OCTOBER

(Confederation of African Football (CAF) Silver Jubilee Cup, Cairo)
Zambia 5 Egypt 3, Zambia 0 Egypt 0

(Africa Cup Winners' semi-finals first leg)
Power Dynamos 2, Djoliba (Senegal) 1

Return Leg:
Dynamos 0 Djoliba 0

NOVEMBER

(Cup Winners' Final, first leg – Kitwe)
Power dynamos 0 Arab Contractors (Egypt) 2

DECEMBER

Return Leg:
Dynamos 0 Contractors 2

MARCH 1983

(Africa cup Winners' first round, first leg – Lusaka)
Green Buffaloes 5 Maxaquene (Mozambique) 1

Return Leg:
Buffaloes 1 Maxaquene 1

(Africa Cup of Champion Clubs first round, first leg)
Nkana Red Devils 2 Mbabane Highlanders (Swaziland) 2

Return Leg:
Nkana 1 Highlanders 0

APRIL

(Africa Cup of Nations first round (Khartoum Sudan)
Zambia 1 Sudan 2

Zambia was eliminated on 1-2 aggregate

MAY

(Africa Cup Winners)
Green Buffaloes, 2 Sotema (Madagascar) 0.

Return Leg:
Buffaloes 0 Sotema 0

(Africa Cup of Champion Clubs second round, first leg :)
Nkana 4, Pan African (Tanzania) 0.

Return Leg:
Nkana 4, Pan African 2 (post-match penalties)

(Rothmans International Cup)
(Ivory Coast)
Power Dynamos 2, Stella FC 1
Dynamos 4 FC 105 (Gabon) 1
Dynamos 2 Bendel Insurance (Nigeria) 1
Dynamos won the cup after beating Tonnerre Yaoundé of Cameroun 5-4
on post-match penalties.

(International Friendly – Mufulira)
Mufulira Wanderers 4 Pan African 1

AUGUST

(Confederation of Southern African football Association (COSAFA)
Under 20 Cup Tournament – Harare (Inaugural)
Zambia 4, Malawi 0
Zambia 2, Zimbabwe 3
Zambia 5, Zimbabwe 3
Champions: Zambia

SEPTEMBER

Africa Cup Winners' quarter finals, first leg – Lusaka)
Green Buffaloes 1, Horoya (Guinea Conakry) 0

Return Leg:
Buffaloes 0, Horoya 2

(Africa Cup of Champion Clubs quarter finals, first leg – Kitwe)
Nkana Red Devils 4, Villa (Uganda) 0

Return Leg:
Nkana 2 Villa 1

OCTOBER

(Olympic Games second round first leg – Lusaka)
Zambia 1 Egypt 0

Return Leg:
Zambia 0 Egypt 2

(International Women's football – Ndola)
Zambia 0 Zimbabwe 13, Zambia 0 Zimbabwe 4

(Africa Cup of Champion Clubs semi-finals)
First Leg
Nkana Red Devils 0 National (Egypt) 0

NOVEMBER

Second Leg:
Nkana 0 National 2

JANUARY 1984

(East and Central African Inter-Club Challenge Cup Tournament)
Nkana Red Devils 1, Young Africans (Tanzania) 2
Nkana 0, AFC Leopards (Kenya) 0, Nkana 2 Berec (Malawi) 0

FEBRUARY

International Friendly, Lilongwe, Malawi)
Zambia 0 Malawi 1, Zambia 1 Malawi 0

APRIL

(Africa Cup Winners' first round, first leg)
Red Arrows 9, Linare (Lesotho) 1

Return Leg:
Arrows 3 Linare 1

(African Cup Champion Clubs first round, first leg :)
Nkana Red Devils 5 LPF (Lesotho) 0

Second Leg:
Nkana 1 LPF 0

(Africa Cup Winners' second round, first leg :)
Red Arrows 1, Vita of Zaire (now the Democratic Republic of the Congo) 2

Return Leg:
Arrows 1, Vita 0
Arrows qualified on away goals counting double rule.

(African Cup Champion Clubs second round)
First leg Nkana Red Devils 1 National Printing (Somalia) 2

Return Leg:
Nkana 3 National Printing 0

JUNE

(International friendly, Lusaka)
Zambia 1, Zimbabwe 1

JULY

(International friendly, Harare)
Zambia 1, Zimbabwe 2
(International friendly – Lusaka)
Zambia 2, Congo 1

AUGUST

Zambia 'B' 2, Stoke City (English FA side) 1
Zambia 'A' 2 Stoke City 3

World Cup first round)
First Leg:
Zambia 3 Uganda 0
Return Leg:
Zambia 0 Uganda 1

(Africa Cup Winners' Cup)
Red Arrows 2 Al Ahly (Libya) 0
Return Leg:
Arrows 0 Al Ahly 3

(Africa Cup of Champion Clubs quarter-finals)
Nkana Red Devils 1 Zamalek (Egypt) 1
Return Leg:
Nkana 1 Zamalek 5

(Fourth All-Africa Youth cup)
First Leg:
(Maputo) Zambia 3 Mozambique 0
Return Leg:
Zambia 5 Mozambique 0
(Zambia National Commercial Bank Trophy)
Zambia Schools 4 Tanzania Schools 1
Zambia Schools 2 Tanzania Schools 1

NOVEMBER

(World Cup Youth)
Zambia 1 Ethiopia 3

DECEMBER

(ECA Senior Challenge Cup – Uganda)
Zambia 2 Zimbabwe 0
Zambia 2 Tanzania Mainland 1
Zambia 1 Uganda 1
Semi-final: Zambia 2 Kenya 0
Final: Zambia 3 Malawi 0 (Post-match penalties)

JANUARY 1985

(World Cup Under-16 first round)
First leg (Lusaka) Zambia 2 Lesotho 1
Return Leg: Zambia 1 Lesotho 0 (Maseru)

(East and Central African Inter-Club Challenge Cup – Sudan)
Nkana Red Devils 0 Mereikh (Sudan) 0
Nkana 4 Marines (Somalia) 0
Nkana 0 AFC Leopards (Kenya) 4
Nkana 0 KMKM (Zanzibar) 1

FEBRUARY

(International friendlies – Zimbabwe)
Zambia 1 Zimbabwe 1 (Gweru)
Zambia 3 Zimbabwe 2 (Bulawayo)

Matchedje (Mozambique) Tour of Zambia
Nkwazi 0 Matchedje 2 (Lusaka)
Green Buffaloes 3 Matchedje 2 (Livingstone)
Green Eagles 5 Matchedje 0 (Kabwe)

MARCH

(Africa Cup Winners' First round)
First Leg: Mufulira Wanderers 0 Manzini Wanderers (Swaziland) 0
Return Leg: Mufulira Wanderers 2 Manzini 0

(Africa Cup of Champion Clubs first round)
First Leg:
Power Dynamos 4 KMKM (Zanzibar) 0
Return Leg:
Dynamos 2 KMKM 1

(World Cup Under-16 third round)
First Leg: Zambia 2 Congo 0
Return Leg:
Zambia 0 Congo 2
Congo won 4-2 on post-match penalties

(International friendly)
Zambia 1 Malawi 1 (Ndola)
Zambia 2 Malawi 2 (Lusaka)

(World Cup second round first leg)
Zambia 4 Cameroun1

(Africa Cup winners' Cup second round first leg)
Mufulira Wanderers 1 AFC Leopards (Kenya) 1

Return match:
Wanderers lost 3-4 on post-match penalties after a deadlock in Nairobi

MAY
(Africa Cup of Champion Clubs)
Power Dynamos 0 Black Rhinos (Zimbabwe) 2 (Kitwe)
Return Leg:
Dynamos 1 Rhinos 1

JULY
(World Cup third round first leg)
Zambia 0 Algeria 1
Return match:
Zambia 0 Algeria 1

Confederation of Southern African Football Association (COSAFA) Cup
Swaziland
Zambia 3 Botswana 0
Zambia 1 Swaziland 1
Zambia 1 Malawi 2
Zambia was eliminated in the preliminaries.

(City of Lusaka's Tour of Nigeria)
City 0 Enugu Rangers 2

City 1 BBC Lions 1
City 0 Defence Industry 1

AUGUST

(Africa Cup of Nations qualifying series, first leg)

Zambia 0 Nigeria 0
Final qualifying round
Zambia 1 Nigeria 0
Zambia failed to reach the quarter – finals.

OCTOBER

(ECA Senior Challenge Cup – Zimbabwe)
Zambia 2 Malawi 2
Zambia 0 Uganda 3

NOVEMBER

(International Military Sports Council (CISM) Games – Tanzania)
Zambia 3 Zimbabwe 1
Zambia 2 Swaziland 0
Semi-finals:
Zambia 3 Botswana 0
Final:
Zambia 1 Zimbabwe 3 (post match penalties after 1-1 draw)

(International friendly – Zaire (now the Democratic Republic of the Congo)
President Mobutu's 20th Anniversary of power
Zambia 1 Zaire 0
Zambia 1 Cote d'Ivoire 0
Zambia 0 Egypt 1

Cote d'Ivoire won the tournament on a better goal difference than Zambia's after each team lost one game and won two in the four- nation event held in Kinshasa.

JANUARY 1986

(ECA Inter-Club Challenge Cup – Tanzania)

Mufulira Wanderers 1 Gor Mahia (Kenya) 0
Mufulira Wanderers 1 Wagad (Somalia) 0
Mufulira 2 Maji (Tanzania) 0
Semi-finals:
Mufulira Wanderers 2 Young Africans (Tanzania) 4
(Post-match penalties)
Third and fourth place play-offs:
Mufulira Wanderers 0 AFC Leopards (Kenya) 1

FEBRUARY

(International friendlies)
Zambia 6 Botswana 0 (Ndola)
Zambia 3 Botswana 0 (Lusaka)

(Defence Forces friendlies)
Zambia 1 Egypt (Livingstone)
Zambia 2 Egypt 2 (Lusaka)
International friendlies
Zambia 0 Saudi Arabia 1

MARCH

(15th African Cup of Nations finals – Egypt)
Zambia 2 Cameroun 3
Zambia 0 Algeria 0
Zambia 0 Morocco 1

Algeria and Morocco were Africa's representatives at the 1986 World Cup
finals in Mexico.

(Africa Cup Winners' first round, first leg – Bulawayo)
Power Dynamos 3 Bulawayo Highlanders (Zimbabwe) 1

APRIL

Second Leg:
Dynamos 2 Highlanders (Zimbabwe) 0

(Africa Cup of Champion Clubs first round, first leg – Kitwe)
Nkana Red Devils 4 Sotema (Madagascar) 1
Second Leg:

Nkana 1 Sotema 2 (Antananarivo)

(International Schools Competition)
Zambia Schools 1 Kenya Schools 1
Zambia 2 Kenya Schools 4 (post-match penalties).

MAY

(Africa Cup of Winners' Cup second round, first leg – Zanzibar)
Power Dynamos 1 Miembeni 1
Return Leg:
Dynamos 5 Miembeni 0

(Africa Cup of Champion Clubs second round, first leg – Addis Ababa)
Nkana Red Devils 0 Ethiopia Breweries 0

JUNE

Second Leg: Nkana 4 Breweries 3 (penalties)

(Cercle Brugge (Belgium) Tour of Zambia)
Zambia XI 0 Brugge 0
Mufulira Wanderers 1 Brugge 3
Zambia 1 Brugge 4

(Zambia Tour of Malawi – friendlies)
Zambia 2 Malawi 0
Zambia 1 Malawi 0

SEPTEMBER

Under 20 (Under 20 COSAFA Cup tournament – Malawi)
Zambia beat defending Champions Zimbabwe 1-0 in the final to win the
trophy for the second time.
(Africa Cup of Champion Clubs quarter-finals first leg – Kitwe)
Nkana Red Devils 2 Accra Hearts of Oak (Ghana) 0
Second Leg:
Nkana 1 Hearts of Oak 1

International friendlies
Zambia 2 Zaire 2 (Ndola)
Zambia 0 Zaire 1 (Lusaka)

THE ROAD TO SEOUL

The year 1987 was a mixed grill for Zambian soccer. Apparently, the grill was for the better, for the national team was in for a historic feat at the beginning of 1988.

On 31 January 1988, Zambia played with all her heart to gallantly fall 0-1 to Black Stars of Ghana in the final Seoul Olympics qualifier in Accra. The team flew back home to a red carpet welcome, being feted at State House and paraded in Cairo Road in Lusaka before chanting crowds. What more could the boys deserve in terms of a reception for beating Ghana on a 2-1 aggregate after a 2-0 first leg lead registered two weeks earlier at Lusaka's Independence Stadium?

Since it was the final qualifying round of the preliminary competition, victory had earned Zambia passage to Seoul, Republic of Korea, and this was by beating one of Africa's most dreaded sides.

The sweetness of that victory all came from the sourness of the rugged path to it. And since it was unprecedented, Zambian fans were stunned. They could not believe it because they had long stopped believing in football after being disenchanted over and over again by the events of the preceding year from the end of 1986 to December, 1987 especially at international level.

After campaigning for it so fervently at international level and finally being awarded the privilege of hosting the 1988 African Nations cup finals, Zambia withdrew. Towards the end of 1986, Government announced the decision to withdraw from hosting the tournament due to financial constraints.

Zambia won 3-1, against Malawi in April in Lusaka in the first leg for the All-Africa Games in Kenya in August. Although beaten, 2-0 in Blantyre, Malawi were through to the finals in Nairobi on the away-goals.

FAZ took another gamble by entering the Olympic Games competition in which Zambia were drawn against Botswana in the first preliminary round. Zambia won 7-0 on aggregate in June.

Zambia were to face their first real hurdle, the Uganda Cranes, who had triumphed in the previous encounters, mainly in the East and Central African Senior Challenge Championship Cup series. In the first leg in Kampala, Uganda won 2-1 with no Zambian professionals featured.

On 15 November, exactly one month after the first leg, Samuel 'Zoom' Ndhlovu, Freddie Mwila and Godfrey Chitalu sat shoulder to shoulder on the Zambian bench as the local boys, spurred on by the recalled Stone Nyirenda and Johnstone Bwalya, overhauled Uganda 5-0.

Rallying fans looked bewitched as it was too good to be true. Their utterances were incoherent and their vision blurred by tears of ecstasy. The calculated turns of Nyirenda and the bustling mettle of Bwalya, combined with the local finesse of Wisdom Chansa, Ashios Melu, Frederick Kashimoto, Richard Siame, Fighton Simukonda and goalkeeper extra-ordinary, Efford Chabala, drove the terraces to a rumbling sensual bliss.

Now the public tune changed to a conservative call against the changing of the national team line-up.

The battle was still raging on and the real war was yet to be met head on. Zambia's moment of truth was yet to come with the Black Stars lurking menacingly at the next corner.

At that time, FAZ had slowly regained its lost pride as the fans shyly restored their confidence in the soccer body. But FAZ would not live to put its foes to shame. The National Sports Council of Zambia dissolved the entire FAZ Executive Committee and handled all the football affairs pending the appointment of an interim FAZ Executive.

The NSCZ continued from where FAZ had left and sent a reshuffled team to the 1987 ECA Senior Championship in Ethiopia in December. It was a disaster and a dark cloud hovered above the soccer fraternity as it squinted through the filmy path to distant Seoul via Accra. Zambia had slumped 0-4 to Uganda Cranes and drew 2-2 with young Zimbabwe to drop out of the race. They came back home to dread fast approaching tango with the Black Stars in January.

And Ghana came, as black as a star can ever be, shining with a mysterious confidence that had tamed the Zambians in all the previous encounters at both club and national levels. But this time to Accra after losing 2-0 on 17 January in Lusaka.

Stone Nyirenda was not there but the other four professionals from Europe led the team to victory.

Zambia scored through Wisdom Chansa and Kalusha Bwalya. History had been inscribed in the annals of African soccer and it did not need to be repeated in Accra a fortnight later when Zambia conceded a lone goal. It was too late for plunging stars. Zambia had triumphed, with Johnstone Bwalya, a professional winger, reinforcing the defence and Nyirenda and Msiska calling the juggling tunes up front in the return leg.

Figure 1: Soccer referees paying their respects to the national team, officials, aircrew and a journalist who died in an air disaster on 28 April 1993. This solemn occasion is taking place in Lusaka's Independence Stadium, Zambia.

Figure 2: Striker Collins Mbesuma (second, from left) missing a header in a match played at Nchanga Stadium in Chingola.

Figure 3: Zambia and Mufulira Wanderers goalkeeper
extraordinary, Efford Chabala.

Figure 4: Kelvin Mutale of Zambia (left) in a tussle.

Figure 5: Gone but not forgotten: Alex Chola (left) and Godfrey Chitalu coached the national team that perished in an air disaster in 1993.

Figure 6: Zambia and 'Magnificent' Kabwe Warriors goalking Godfrey 'Ucar' Chitalu (behind) during an international encounter at the Independence Stadium in Lusaka, Zambia.

Figure 7: Zambia and Mufulira Wanderers star Kalusha Bwalya (left) leaving for his first professional soccer career in Europe. He is currently Football Association of Zambia (FAZ) President.

Figure 8: Samuel 'Zoom Ndhlovu, former Zambia
and Mufulira Wanderers coach.

Figure 9: Zambian striker Godfrey 'Ucar' Chitalu (in hat)
leading national team-mates on arrival in Lusaka, Zambia.

Figure 10: Then Football Association of Zambia (FAZ) President,
Teddy Mulonga (left), confers with his Executive Committee
during the Annual General Meeting. He is currently the Permanent
Secretary – Ministry of Sport, Youth and Child Development.

Figure 12: Defender Ashios Melu of Zambia and
Mufulira Wanderers Football Club.

Figure 13: Kabwe Warriors' midfielder Boniface Simutowe
receiving the Footballer of the Year national award.

CRICKET

Zambian freelance journalist Haroon Ghumra, in 1985 highlighted the bleak future of cricket in the country, although the governing cricket body deserves praise for running the existing structure successfully. It has been raising enough money every year to send the national team to participate in East and Central African (ECA) Quadrangular tournament. Writing in the ZAMBIA DAILY MAIL newspaper, Ghumra, however, said that gone are days when schools used to participate in the various leagues and other competitions. When one looks back one discovers with awe that even secondary schools like Kamwala and Kabulonga Boys (both of Lusaka), which had great cricketing potential are now but a tearful shadow of their former selves. Kamwala produced cricketers of the calibre of the left arm spinner Bipin Desai, all rounder Majid Pandor, hard hitting Subhas Devalia, versatile Solly Patel and Yunus Dudhia, who were capped for the national team.

Phil Edmunds, the brilliant slow left arm spinner who went on to win international honours by being capped for England, and former Zambian star Krish Patel, both learnt their cricket at Kabulonga (then Gilbert Rennie Secondary School). Ghumra asked 'Who then is playing cricket at the present moment in Zambia? It is not surprising to note that only those that played cricket previously are continuing to do so. The other group comprises children of former players and fans and expatriates.'

The primary concern of the nation's cricket policy-makers today must surely be to have the game resurrected at the grassroots level and to find ways of capturing the imagination of indigenous Zambian youths. Ghumra gave a four-point plan which should entail the introduction in Zambia of softball cricket at the primary school level, appropriate authorities, club sponsorship scheme for indigenous Zambians and hard-ball cricket in secondary schools. All that is needed is a small area with a short marking, a simple bat or a piece of wood to act as such, an empty drum or a box if stumps are not available and tennis or other rubber ball.

A crash course on the basic principles of the game for the sports teachers, conducted by the respective district associations affiliated to the Zambia Cricket Union (ZCU), should ensure that softball cricket gets off the ground. Roan Antelope Cricket Club in Luanshya trained one schoolboy Zed Rusike, who ultimately made the national grade. Similarly two boys, Moses Zwiya and Kwaleyela Ikafa were sponsored by Nondescripts Cricket Club of Lusaka in the early seventies. The present ZCU executive, no doubt, has the unenviable role of reintroducing a combined effort from all concerned. 'Let not the future generation say that we hastened the death of this great game in Zambia,' Ghumra says.

Major Hughes Collins, patron of the East African Cricket Conference, supported Ghumra's view that cricket like any other game must be started at an early age and his idea of its introduction. In the form of softball cricket, was the ideal answer for this form of cricket. It was cheap and not dangerous. 'It is thus my real wish that cricket, like association football, may become a part of life in Zambia and that all school headmasters both primary and secondary, may agree to introduce this game into their schools.' Maj. Collins said.

Cricket in Zambia began at the turn of the century being the chief recreation for the colonialists. As such it remained in a crude form until sophistication set into the society, and the gradual evolution into very competitive leagues at the height of white supremacy in the then Northern Rhodesia from the fifties onwards. The great post-war copper boom brought prosperity to Northern Rhodesia especially on the Copperbelt because of the splendid and beautiful playgrounds, schools and other facilities that were being built by the various mining towns for their workers. An era of improved standards for all the different sport that Zambia's gorgeous weather was being ushered in. The capital city, too, shared in this attitude but whereas the facilities were prepared on the Copperbelt, clubs in Lusaka had to stand on their own. This resulted in inferior facilities as compared to those on the Copperbelt. This marked difference was also very apparent in the results when the two provinces met in any sport. The Copperbelt usually emerged the victors. Indeed this is true even today in most sporting activities. The superiority by the Copperbelt had direct bearing on the composition of the national teams where the majority of the squad's members mainly came from the Copperbelt, a stranglehold that has occasionally been broken.

Similarly, representation at Federal level bore a great resemblance to that of Northern Rhodesia's in which the Rhodesian team (as it was known) comprised chiefly sportsmen and sportswomen from the Mashonaland and Matabeleland areas. Northern Rhodesia, more or less was an integral part of the Manicaland or the Midlands of Southern Rhodesia (Zimbabwe) when it came to selections into the federal cricket team. For a player from Northern Rhodesia to make it into the Rhodesian squad he had to be twice as good as his Southern Rhodesian counterpart. This equation when translated meant that a Lusaka based sportsman had to be twice as good as his Copperbelt colleague in order to earn a place in the Northern Rhodesia team.

It was virtually impossible for non-white sportsmen to win selection. If they did, they had to maintain peak form throughout as the slightest excuse was always sought to reinstate the status quo. The earliest penetration into the realms of cricket in Zambia was made by Yusuf 'Pathan' Patel, a high school teacher at Prince Philip (now Kamwala Secondary School) in Lusaka. He retired from active cricket in 1985 after a career that spanned thirty years.

Patel cannot remember how many hundreds he made except that he made sixteen in one season with two not outs in the 80's and 90's during the 1963/64 season. His feat earned him historically the first ever sports man of the year award. He remembers this award with nostalgia as it was his first contact with any of Zambia's nationalists because the presentation was done by Simon Mwansa Kapwepwe.

Although Yusuf 'Pathan' Patel was a self-taught athlete of remarkable prowess, he strongly advocates the school system with proper coaches to inculcate 'sound technique.' This in itself could be the base from which all sorts of improvisations could then be made. His name must be cherished in Zambia today not merely for cricket, a game where he set such high glided standards, but for being the epitomy of the ideal sportsman who glided above race, colour and creed. He is a person who has always brandished the torch of fairplay.

Patel was a product of Loughborough college of Physical Education in England. He has excelled at several sports with a sound working knowledge of all the other games, because he taught sport as well as class at Prince Philip High School. He represented the non-white Rhodesian cricket in the late fifties and played for Matabeleland Coloureds in the Bulawayo region at soccer before moving to Lusaka in 1960 to enroll with the all-conquering City of Lusaka football team under Jack Sewell. An ankle injury inflicted by a Broken Hill (Kabwe) Warriors defender ended Patel's football career in 1962 before he began his famous exploits on the cricket field. If all the current fine players and those of yesteryear can tender a fraction back to cricket and whatever else they played just as Patel gave himself totally, sport will definitely be better off. He was a backseat observer whose presence was seen at major sporting events and whose only regret is that he cannot spare the time to 'give back to golf a game he began late in life that gives him much pleasure. Incidentally he is a steady single figure handicap player.

He has scored a century on every major ground from Chipata to Livingstone. Patel was the object of ridicule when the first attempt was made to Zambianise the national cricket team in 1974. Under his captaincy in Dar-es-Salaam in 1974 an extremely modest Zambian team humbled all East African opposition that opened the eyes of administrators to endeavour to experiment and gave him the last laugh.

After the attainment of independence in October 1964, Zambia severed sporting links with Rhodesia as a result of Unilateral Declaration of Independence (UDI) by the latter. The cricket administrators had to look elsewhere for competitions. In 1966 an East African team comprising players from Kenya, Tanzania and Uganda toured Zambia. Zambia successfully affiliated to the East African Cricket Conference which organized annual tournaments among member countries. The participating countries, before Zambia was affiliated, were Kenya, Tanzania and Uganda.

The tournament competed for is the present Sir Robert Menzies Trophy. Zambia first hosted the competition in 1969 and that was the year the country won the trophy as well. Kenya dominated the competition by winning it on many occasions. After 1980, Kenya affiliated to the International Cricket Conference as an associate member and ceased participating in the tournament. Zambia also won the ECA competition held in Tanzania in 1974, whose team composed entirely of Zambia nationals. That success was repeated in 1979 in Kenya, and since then Zambia has maintained a stronghold on the Sir Robert Menzies Trophy. Participation in the ECA quadrangular tournament which now includes Malawi, has given opportunity to various cricketers from Zambia to feature in the Mini World Cup and the ICC Trophy competitions played in England, as a member of the East African squads.

International competition has also been provided by some Indian and English Country sides. These featured Test players and gave spectators ample opportunity to enjoy and appreciate the game of cricket. In 1983 Zambia played host to East Africa and Zimbabwe in the first Triangular tournament. Zimbabwe won convincingly.

On the Zambian scene, Southern Province has entered the inter-district competitions after an absence of many years and Mfuwe Sports Club of Chipata is achieving success in the Midlands cup competitions. People who have played the game can return and play an important role either as coaches, administrators or umpires. Despite difficulties, Zambia won the Sir Robert Menzies Trophy in 1969 in Lusaka, 1974 (Dar), 1979 (Nairobi), 1980 (Lusaka), 1981 (Dar), 1982 (Blantyre), 1983 (Ndola/Luanshya), 1985 (Lusaka) and 1986 (Blantyre).

At the club level, Metropolitans of Lusaka participated in the annual Tarmahomed Abdulgani Memorial Tournament (TAGT) against teams from

Malawi, Kenya, Zimbabwe and Tanzania. The competition was incepted in Zambia. The tenth edition was hosted by Metropolitans in April 1987.

Looking back at the TAGT, Patel said the tournaments can also boast of many close contests. The first event played in Lusaka in 1980 and the eventual winners took everybody by surprise. Nobody expected Yusuf Meman's Harare boys to win since they came with a depleted side, but sound application in all departments and effective captaining won the day for Universals from Zimbabwe. December 1982 saw the second TAGT of that year in Dar because Easter 1983 would have been East African's rainy season. If ever a team lost a match on the last lap it was Union of Dar on their home ground. Again the Zimbabweans could not muster a fully strong team and sent a mixture of youth, experience and have beens on tour. It was the latter that pulled them out of the fire in a most historic win.

Tanzania's Union made 211 for 5 on the slow Burhani ground. The stalwarts of their innings were Bashir Tejani, with a sparkling seventy-five and a powerful fifty-five not out from Muneer Shariff. Babu Meman and Sadiq Dudhia each took two wickets. Universals began their chase in grand style. with a quick fire forty-nine first wicket partnership between Sadiq Dudhia and Craig Hodgson. The Bashir Tejani then struck and had Dudhia caught behind the very next over and then successfully sent back Babu Meman and brother and skipper Yusuf Meman for zero's. Universals were suddenly four for forty-nine and appeared destined for doom. Abdul Umerjee and Ebrahim Essop then got together. Slowly and steadily they took the sting out of Union's attack before surmounting their own attack.

The spectators were unbelieving that a good Union attack could so easily be repelled. Abdul Umerjee was bowled with the score at 138 and Universals were still nearly eight runs short with no renowned batsmen to come. First, Ahmed Ebrahim Suleman, and then Rafig Adam stayed with 'old man' Billy and off the third last ball Universals Zimbabwe got home by one run with two balls to spare. What a game that was.

There was absolutely no standing space around the entire ground. This was cricket as it should be. As for Ebrahim Essop who has always been the keenest of players this was perhaps the most fitting moment. This might have been his last big game because of age creeping up, but his beautifully timed six to mid-wicket off Yusuf Ammer will be the treasure of that game. The fifth TAGT moved to Lusaka in 1983 where there were three excellent matches, a rare happening when really there is only one match per tournament that outshines the rest. The year will also be lamented for the fact that the talented all rounder Bill Bourne (winner of the 1979 Sportsman of the Year award in Zambia), was not allowed to participate because of the tournament rules. Consequently Universals Zimbabwe had to withdraw from the tournament when they should have shown the TAGT the way with their array of fine and widely experienced players.

All sporting competitions such as TAGT are purely and simply lessons in public relationship which is what life is. Universals of Kenya finally won the competition in a thrilling finish. For the first time, Kenya were hosts in 1984. As usual there was a lot of interest from the other four teams to play their best teams as everybody wanted to go to lovely Nairobi. Two matches played there were really outstanding. One for the greatest upset that time in the TAGT and next when a third decided the first two, Zimbabwe were perhaps at their strongest ever and took Malawi's Mpingwe for granted in their final match of that tour. Malawi batted first and thanks to fine innings from all-star rounder skipper Vally Tarmohamed they put together a respectful 150. Zimbabwe began as usual very confident and little recklessly at that. Their slightest errors were nearly snapped up by Mpingwe and in two ticks Universals were up against it – six down for fifty and only Babu Meman was sure of himself. Yusuf Patel recalls: 'The alarm bells were ringing all round the dressing rooms and the ground as last hope in big Zahid Abdulla took the crease still eight or fifty runs behind.'

This very gifted sportsman played very confidently. He hit everything loose with great might and accuracy both over and under the ropes. Smiles began to emerge from the Zimbabwean quarters. Afternoon tea eased the mounting tension and all types of advice started being given during the break on how to achieve the remaining twenty-five runs to the last pair who were now batting with great authority. On resumption, alas, the inevitable happened. Abdulla immediately skied a pitched up delivery straight towards the screen and as the ball failed to clear the boundary the waiting fielder gleefully accepted the catch – Mpingwe had performed the impossible. They had beaten one of the finest sides ever fielded in a TAGT by eighteen runs. This heroic act threw the series wide open. A Zambian victory at a good run rate could assure them victory. A Kenyan victory would give them the trophy. A slower win for Zambia would make Zimbabwe the winners. What an amazing eternal triangle.

All the spectators from the Malawi/Zimbabwe game now rushed to the fully thronged Sir Allie Ground, where also tension was beginning to mount. Kenya had already batted making exactly three runs more than they had in Lusaka the year before -199. Their chief architect was a beautifully put together fifty by Azhar Ali with fair contribution from the rest of his team. If Metros (Zambia) would make this score in forty-eight overs then their run rate would win them the TAGT and they set out cautiously. Inayat Bagas and Tarzan Patel held together the middle order. If anybody could accelerate the scoring, these two were the men. Accurate bowling and nerves completely subdued the normally aggressive TARZAN and all hopes of a win within forty-eight overs faded fast. The victory was the next aim although this would have given Zimbabwe the cup. Metros suddenly had new fans – all the Zimbabwe squad and supporters.

Inayat Bagas played his finest innings ever witnessed that day. He was eventually put for seventy-eight. Metros needed four off the last ball in near darkness to win the match and a lovely hit by Yusuf Chhadat which was on its way over the boundary was beautifully caught once again giving Kenya win over Zambia by three runs – 199 to 196.

It was back to Harare for the Easter of 1985. This time Universals Zimbabwe completely whitewashed everybody on their home ground. It was a question of who was the second best. There were no exciting matches that year except for the fact that Metros recorded their first win over Universals Kenya and responding one at that. Kenya were skittled out for a paltry seventy-five which Metros got for the loss of five wickets. Another feature was a superb knock of sixty-nine by Haroon Bagas in only twenty-eight balls against Union for Metros. His timing that day was a joy to behold, especially the towering sixes between mid off and mid wicket.

Another feature was the first hat-trick recorded in the TAGT at that moment by Mpingwe captain Iqbal Lorgat against Metros. In 1986, Malawi were the hosts. No fireworks or scores were recorded although the match between the two best teams Universals Kenya and Universals Zimbabwe provided the usual nail biting finish. In a very slow scoring match, on a slow wicket and very wet outfield, Universals thinking this to be a mere formality confidently strode to the wicket and off a had first ball lost their opener and all the others followed suit in regular procession.

Some out to good balls, others run outs and yet others to bad shots. Whilst wages were changing with every falling wicket, Azar Ali the seasoned left hander kept his cool and was prepared to take his runs at leisure. He was in no hurry to get the match over and gradually the score crept up into the desired 60's and when a delivery was pitched up to him he gently put it over the bowler's head and called 'two.' His timing was so good and sweet that the ball carried sight screen for six. The match was over seventy-two to sixty-nine in Kenya's favour.

In Dar-es-Salaam in 1986, there was only one talking point, and it was the match between Universals Kenya and Universals Zimbabwe. On a slow outfield Zimbabwe made 186 which at the outset was a winning total within bounds of a reasonably accurate bowling. The chief run getters being skipper Ali Shah and Sikander Abdulla. The Kenyans had contrary views and started to pull themselves, thanks in the main to marvelous superb timing on an awfully slow outfield. His great knock besides being the best in the tournament swung the game completely in Kenya's way. Zahoor Sheikh and tail end partners had just to cruise amiably on to ensure victory, Yusuf Patel said.

Azar Sheikh's little nephew was the mainstay at this stage. He out-scored even the burly Zahoor. Kenya in the last two overs needed six runs to win with three wickets in hand. It looked all over but attempts by Kenya to get two's instead of singles caused two runs outs. Zimbabwe won the championship.

Figure 14: A group picture of Zambia 'B' cricket team in Swaziland.

Figure 15: Yusuf 'Pathan' Patel leads members of the Zambia cricket team on arrival in Lusaka from Nairobi, Kenya, where they played in the 1968 East African tournament.

NETBALL

'Netball is the finest women's team game in the world. This is a bold statement, and one I am prepared to defend. Other team sports undoubtedly have their qualities. I have played and enjoyed many of them – such as athletics – but netball for me will always be the supreme game,' former Netball Association of Zambia (NAZ) secretary, Mavis Muyunda, said.

Before turning to the sport as we know it today, it is worth looking at its origins. It is an offshoot of basketball, the game founded by Dr. James Naismith at Springfield College, Massachusetts in the United States of America. But the great 'leap' to give netball world stature has only been made in the last three decades. In 1960 the Federation of Women's Basketball and Netball Associations (BANA) was formed which later became known as the International Federation of Netball Associations.

Netball can be played by women of all shapes, sizes, and aptitudes, and that is one of the great attractions of local, regional and international tournaments.

Opportunity is a great thing in any sport and netball provides a lot of chances. Certainly there are subscriptions to be paid, but the equipment is virtually a ball, goalposts, a team and some uniforms.

There are three fundamental principles in netball and these are stepping, catching and throwing. Movement is everything in netball – movement for the ball, movement in catching and movement in throwing.

The City of Lusaka Netball Club emanated from the Lusaka Municipal Netball Club which was pioneered by Mavis Lengalenga (now Mrs. Muyunda), Joyce Munyama, Hellen (now Mrs Chabi), Jennipher Kabaso (now Mrs Phiri), Clare Mutepuka and others – most of whom were white expatriates – in 1966. Practice sessions were held at Katombola Sports Club as it was known then. As the game became more organized, with lots more Zambians participating, the club changed its name to City of Lusaka in 1968. In 1975 the Netball Association of Zambia, with Elizabeth Zulu as chairman and Mrs Muyunda as secretary, represented Zambia at the Third World Confederation to which the Netball Association of Zambia was later affiliated. Zambia became the second African country to be affiliated to the Federation. Kenya having been the first.

A point of interest worth mentioning about this conference was that Zambia moved a motion to have BANA suspended from the Federation. She was seconded by Jamaica. The motion was adopted after a heated debate. This could be said to have been the Netball Association of Zambia's first impact at international level.

Since Independence the game of netball has grown in popularity in Zambia. The game is on the upswing mainly due to the efforts of the Netball Association of Zambia. This includes affiliation to the East and Central African Netball Confederation (ECANC).

In November 1976, ten netballers accompanied by eight officials made their debut in the East and Central African Senior Challenge Cup tournament in Iringa, Tanzania. Leading the delegation were NAZ chairman, Elizabeth Zulu, and Mrs Muyunda, a Principal in the Ministry of Finance and later to become a Minister of State in the Ministry of Foreign Affairs. The team consisted of Changu Shankomaune and Veronica Zulu from City of Lusaka N.C.; Anne Mbilika of Nchanga Rangers N.C; Catherine Miyutu of Kabwe Police N.C., Florence Bwalya of Konkola Blades N.C., and Dorothy Besa. Midlands zone officials, Dominic Nzala and Jonathan Halukowa, were the coaches. Colgate Palmolive (Zambia) Limited, apart from sponsoring the trip, ensured that the squad was smartly turned out by donating uniforms, jackets, shoes, socks, track suits, 'chitenge' evening dresses, caps, tee-shirts and travelling bags.

Before departure Mrs Muyunda said, 'From the way things are now I can safely say we stand a good chance of doing well in the tournament.' The competition was held two months after Zambia affiliated to ECANC. Other countries that took part in the competition were Tanzania Mainland, Kenya, Malawi, Lesotho and Zanzibar.

In 1983 Zambia won the ECA Senior Challenge Cup after drawing 28-28 with hosts, Kenya, in Nairobi, after whacking Uganda 37-29. Alice Lwimba (now Mrs Chitafu) of Zambia Steel Netball Club, was voted the Best Player of the tournament, Regina Sikazwe, the Best Umpire and former NAZ General Secretary Betty Muleya, Best Delegate.

In 1995 Zambia played host to the ECA Senior Challenge Cup and retained the Cup in a closely fought competition. They beat Kenya 47-42, Tanzania 42-40, Uganda 38-29 and Malawi 61-19. Zambia topped the scoreboard with eight points followed by Kenya with six, Tanzania with four, Uganda two and Malawi zero. The squad consisted of Priscah Kunda, Never Chambakale, Lucy Mutale, all of Chibuku Warriors Netball Club, Anne Mbilika, Alice Lwimba, Gladys Mwelwa of Zambia Steel Netball Club, Beatrice Mulenga, Ednah Nanyangwe and Daisy Namwila of ZESCO Ndola Netball Club, Aggie Chewe, Regina Sokoni of Zamsure Netball Club, Estellah Chileshe of Profund Warriors Netball Club and Gertrude Shanaube of Green Baffaloes Netball Club. Eddie Nkondo was coach. Shanaube was co-opted into the squad at virtually the last minute.

Other major international commitments included the hosting of the 1978 ECA Senior Challenge Cup tournament and participation in the Supreme Council for Sport in Africa Zone Six Championships in 1981 in Harare, Zimbabwe.

At club level, Zesco Ndola made its debut in the East and Central African Cup tournament in 1985 staged in Tanzania. Zesco Ndola finished second to hosts, Bora, having beaten Malawi's Civil Service 61-11 and Kenya Breweries 47-45.

In 1982, Zambia finished second to Kenya in the ECA Senior Challenge Cup in Nairobi. Much of the success could be attributed to Colgate Palmolive (Zambia) Limited which has assisted NAZ on many occasions.

Former NAZ Secretary, Betty Muleya said, 'The success of NAZ is due to the support rendered by different individuals, such as the late Sports Director, Musa Kasonka and Julio Chiluba.

Netball derives no financial gains in terms of gate takings because the game is played in the open. Nevertheless, the future of netball in Zambia is bright. A lot of companies sponsor different clubs and with such support, the standards will continue to improve, Muleya voted general secretary in 1974, and who originated from the famous City of Lusaka Netball Club, said she has had some sad moments, 'especially when I seem to have a blackout when pondering the future of an organization such as NAZ.' Muleya resigned and replaced by Midlands Netball Association (MINA) Fixtures Secretary, Lillian Nkhuwa.

Figure 16: Netball in Zambia is a popular sport and played
by all ages. Above, is action in the Midlands.

Figure 17: Zambia and Nchanga Rangers
goal-shooter Anne Mbilika (left) is beaten to the ball.

Figure 18: 'No! this is my ball!', the netballer on the
left seems to be saying as opponents close in.

Figure 19: Netball thrills are common in Zambia.

VOLLEYBALL

Volleyball has become of the most popular sport played by the Zambian youth. On statistics, it is second only to soccer. It is a sport which is played by both males and females. Its simplicity merely promotes it much further in terms of cost. An area of eighteen metres by nine and a net with two poles of three metres in length is all that is required to play the game.

Today almost every secondary school has a volleyball team and three out of every five primary schools have a volleyball court.

Volleyball like many other sports has physical, mental and social benefits for individuals as well as for the society. This is why a trace of events on its development should be kept.

History of Volleyball

1895 — Volleyball was initiated in Holyoke, Massachusetts, United States of America by Dr. William C. Morgan. At this time the sport was called 'Mintonette' and eventually changed to 'Volleyball' by Dr. Halstead of Springfield, United States of America, because the game was basically designed as a recreation activity for businessmen and was highly popular at summer resorts and playgrounds throughout the United States.

1900 — Canada became the first foreign country to adopt the sport. The international YMCA movement was instrumental in spreading the popularity of volleyball throughout the world. It was played for the first time in Cuba in 1905; Peru in 1910; Uruguay in 1912, and Brazil in 1917.

In Asia, popular belief is that volleyball was first reported from India in 1900 and the Philippines in 1910.

1913 — The First Asian Games with participation of volleyball teams from China, Japan and the Philippines were held in this year.

1917 – Europe was first exposed to volleyball during the First World War. Volleyball spread to different countries such as France in 1917, Yugoslavia in 1918, Czechoslovakia and Poland in 1919 and the Soviet Union in 1922.

Volleyball was introduced in Africa in 1923.

The style of playing and rules were developed differently in each section and nation of the world. In Asia, because of the stature of the population, Far Eastern rules were geared to these characteristics. For example, there were nine players per team rather than six and the games called for no side-outs, no rotation order, two attempts at a service and a wider court. The height of the net was also lowered approximately (15.24 centimetres). These Asian rules are still being used, but this game is losing its popularity in favour of the six-man game.

Attempts to organize an International Federation were made in Stockholm in 1934 and at the Olympic Games in Berlin in 1936. Another attempt was made in Prague in 1946, which was an initial success. The International Volleyball Federation finally came into being on 20 April, 1947 on the initiative to which fourteen national federations were affiliated. From that time to 1984 its President was Paul Libaud, followed by Ruben Acosta. From 1947 to 1978 there were in excess of 140 nations affiliated to the International Volleyball Federation.

Volleyball gained still further popularity after the Second World War in Europe.

The Japanese Volleyball Association has since 1960 made a major contribution to the development of the game in the world. Each year top Japanese teams tour the world competing against other top countries as well as playing exhibition games for the development of the game throughout the world. There are today perhaps over a hundred and fifty registered volleyball players.

In addition to the ever increasing popularity of the game, the level of play of top international volleyball is increasing rapidly. From one world championship – the first being held in Prague in 1949, with ten nations competing – to the next, and one Olympic Games to the next, the level of play is improving.

Volleyball is a game which can be played at a high competitive level by intensely trained athletes. It is also outstanding as a recreational sport because it has the following recreational principles:

- It is an interesting game, easy to learn and enjoyable to play. It is cheap, requiring only simple equipment and facilities. A prepared ground is not necessary. It is a non-contact sport thus reducing the danger of personal injury. It is a 'team' sport which enhances the enjoyment of team play. It can be played by all ages and both sexes, either separately or together.

- It can be played indoors as well as outdoors. As a sport of physical education volleyball promotes competitive spirit and positive qualities of character development.

- It can be highly competitive, requiring a high level of personal fitness and training or can be relaxing in a high enjoyable recreational activity. Therefore, volleyball is extremely popular and is played in many places such as elementary and high schools, universities, in the army, the factory, on the farm, in parks, on beaches and a at several other places for recreational purposes.

- The great adaptability of volleyball has allowed each national Federation, League or even each game to be played by simplified rules according to the desires and objectives of the participants.

The development of Volleyball in Zambia has a very interesting history with varying opinions.

The fact is that volleyball was first introduced to Zambia, then Northern Rhodesia, by the Indian community around 1955. The sport was then played with very minimum restrictions as far as the rules of the game were concerned. The sport was played merely as recreation for the families in certain communities. The capital city Lusaka first experienced the boom of the sport in Indian community centres, of which Lotus Club is a very important landmark.

In 1960 the army and police forces cottoned onto the game, so to speak, and competitive volleyball was introduced to the country. This introduction of the game to the defence forces dictated the need to conform to the rules.

The next stage was the introduction of the game to colleges, with Evelyn Hone College in Lusaka being the first institution of higher learning to participate in the sport. This precipitated the germination of the sport in other institutions of learning, with the lower limit being secondary schools.

By 1965 the game was being played extensively on the line of rail up to the Copperbelt. This popularity called for an organizing committee of some kind. Dev Babbar became the Administrative Committee's first chairman in 1968 and the year marked the beginning of organized volleyball in Zambia.

To try and understand the development of the sport thereafter I will restrict myself to important features which are worth noting in the history of volleyball in Zambia.

From August to September 1973 the first International Volleyball Coaches course for Africa was held in Lusaka. Malawi, Ghana, Sierra Leone, Ethiopia, Liberia, the Gambia, Uganda and Zambia were represented.

In 1976 the Buffaloes team from the army hit peak form in volleyball. The team was unbeaten for four years running from 1974 to 1977. The men behind this success were Captain Elias Ngosa (coach), Obby Chibafwa 'Powerhouse' and Teddy Habanyama, 'left handed bomber.' These are just a few of what made up the Buffaloes team. In the same year Buffaloes represented Zambia in Libya.

The year 1977 saw the emergence of two teams to challenge Buffaloes. These were the University of Zambia (UNZA) and Indeni. UNZA had just, acquired a new coach Francis Sichande, while Indeni had Lenzo Vanni from Italy. This year also witnessed the end of the Buffaloes' stranglehold on volleyball. They were beaten by UNZA. Teddy Habanyama joined Indeni from Buffaloes but reducing Buffaloes' strength. The coach Captain Elias Ngosa, was also transferred to Kabwe. The 1978 final was a battle between UNZA and Indeni.

In 1978 a team sponsored by Zambia Breweries emerged on the volleyball scene. Some players from Indeni, Buffaloes and mainly from Matero Boys Secondary School students in Lusaka formed a team which became quite a force to reckon with. Players like George Kasanda, Hamby Kalanga (formerly of Indeni) and Teddy Habanyama were the backbone of this team. UNZA volleyball team travelled to Nairobi, Kenya, for the African Inter-University Games.

The University of Zambia team travelled to Mexico for the World University Games. In June, Serenje, for the first time, saw first class volleyball being played at a tournament organized by Andy Lorryman, then national coach.

In the same year Zambia hosted the Zone VI tournament in Kitwe at which three countries – Zambia, Madagascar and Mauritius. Madagascar won the championship. John Kerrie Maluti, the UNZA setter, became a household name. He was nicknamed 'the Brain' by his fans. The year also witnessed tremendous improvements in the system and tactics of play.

In 1982 an Executive Committee was elected to office with Dev Babbar as leader, Benson Mwewa (Secretary) and T. Musonda (Treasurer). National coach Andy Lorryman later changed hands with Francis Sichande, Indeni participated in the Jamhuri Tournament in Kenya. The Zambia national team toured Zimbabwe for a series of games which they won.

In 1984 Francis Sichande was appointed National coach on his return from the United States of America where he had gone for further studies. The Zambia National team went to Zimbabwe to participate in the Zone VI tournament, which saw participation by Malawi, Zimbabwe and Zambia. Zambia won the trophy for the first time. The Bank of Zambia became a powerhouse in Volleyball.

In 1985 the Bank of Zambia team participated in the Jamhuri Tournament in Nairobi, Kenya, with most of the young talented volleyball players joining the team, Bank of Zambia was almost unbeaten. Indeni's prowess had diminished and Buffaloes began to regain past glory.

By 1986 the Buffaloes team had been rebuilt and was at the top again. There were reflections of problems in the Bank of Zambia team. Indeni suspended further participation in tournaments until an improvement had been made in performance. Butondo Women's volleyball team became champions for two consecutive years, taking over from the University of Zambia.

To detail the history of volleyball without mentioning the Zambia Schools Volleyball Association would be to reflect a distorted image. Special people in the development of volleyball in schools include Father A. Jansen of Lusaka's Matero Boys Secondary School, under whose hands most of the stars of today have passed, and Andy Lorryman, whose tireless efforts to see volleyball grow had always been fruitful. Lorryman was ZAVA chairman.

Black Zambians in then Northern Rhodesia knew the game of volleyball as far back as the 1940's. They did not, however, know it as a competitive sport but rather as a physical fitness exercise in the armed forces during the Second World War.

Former ZAVA general secretary, Stewart Zimba, notes that it was not until early 1960's that the game spread into few schools, colleges and other open clubs. Between 1960 and 1966 volleyball became more and more popular.

In 1968, Dev Babbar of Lusaka formed ZAVA which meant that volleyball was introduced in almost all the secondary schools and colleges. ZAVA held its first annual general meeting in Lusaka in July 1968 to discuss the constitution and elect officials.

Babbar was the Executive Officer for Africa for the International Volleyball

Association (IVF). He is also a former secretary of the Kenya Volleyball Association, and was behind the introduction of volleyball in that country.

In 1963, Babbar criticized the International Olympic Committee (IOC) for its decision to exclude volleyball from the Mexico Olympics. The decision created a lot of anger among the 81 member countries of the IVF, founded in 1949, he said.

In 1964, Babbar was one of the three people who drafted the memorandum which was submitted to the IOC council meeting held in Lausanne, Switzerland, and the men's volleyball was re-instated for the Mexico Olympic Games.

When he formed ZAVA, Babbar's wish was to send a volleyball team to take part in the African championships in Bamako, Mali, in 1969.

On 19 December, 1974 the Ndola Amateur Volleyball League was formed, and was the first of its kind in the country. The officials were Stewart Zimba as chairman and Misheck Mwale, secretary. The formation of the league inspired the executive committee to form the Copperbelt Volleyball Association.

Revival of ZAVA

The meeting to revive the association was held at the Dominican Convent Secondary School in Ndola on 12 May, 1975. Delegates were drawn from the Ndola Amateur Volleyball League, individuals from Kitwe and a representative from the Ministry of Labour and Social Services in Lusaka.

At the end, an interim committee was sworn in consisting of Emilio Panatela (chairman), Zimba (vice-chairman), Ajanta Patel (secretary) and Isaiah Lukanganyama (treasurer). The committee was confirmed in its position at a meeting called by the Ministry of Labour and Social Services in Lusaka on 25 May, 1975. The committee's term ended in September 1976 when elections were held at Hotel Edinburgh in Kitwe.

All the positions were retained unopposed. Director of Sports, Musa Kasonka (late), chaired the meeting.

In 1976, the Copperbelt Amateur Volleyball Association was under the chairmanship of Wilbroad Mutoka and Mizzie Mutambo (secretary). Palatella and Zimba were advisors to the committee. It was during the same year that the Midlands Volleyball Association was formed with Ngalama Kalaluka, then at the University of Zambia, as secretary.

Zimba recalled: "During this period, volleyball had been spread throughout the country and being played even in primary schools."

It was during this year that Zambia hosted the East and Central African (ECA) tournament at Rokana Club in Kitwe. The ZAVA national team also took part in the Africa championships in Libya in 1977. In 1979, another ZAVA general election was held in Kitwe where Palatella was retained as chairman, Zimba (general secretary) and Stephen Banda (treasurer). Hastings Kapepula was elected chairman of the Copperbelt Amateur Volleyball Association, Mutambo (secretary) and Benson Mwewa (fixtures secretary). Volleyball was at its peak in Zambia during this period.

By December 1981, Zimba resigned as ZAVA general secretary and Director of Sports Ngalama Kalaluka dissolved the committee and appointed an interim executive comprising Palatella (chairman) and Mwewa, general secretary. Other members were: Emmanuel Chipofya and Stephen Banda. From 1981, volleyball has progressed with notable teams like Indeni and Bank of Zambia (Ndola) representing the country in both North and East African competitions.

Volleyball which was merely seen as a means of keeping fit has now grown to be a competitive sport, and now legally affiliated to the world body and the Africa Volleyball Confederation.

POLO

The Zambia Polo Association came into being on 9 June, 1966 with Lusaka Polo and Hunt Club, Nkana Polo Club and the Mazabuka Turf Club – Polo Section, being founder club members.

Polo was most probably introduced into the then Northern Rhodesia after the Second World War, when former British officers in the Indian Army settled in the country. These players encouraged farmers and businessmen to take up the sport, and the game was played in Lusaka and Nkana/Kitwe. Names to be remembered from the past are Colonel Ronnie Critchley, Captain Michael Lafone, Major 'Squire' Beeston – Bancroft, Oliver Heywood-Jones, J.J. Potgieter and his son Monty, Jackie Murray, Chester Dean, Clarrie Stakeby-Lewis and Bill Zunkel of Lusaka. On the Copperbelt players of note were Jimmy Dunbar, Des Page, Patsy Coetzee, Ralph and Roy Rixon, Tommy Hammond and Cedric Oates.

Unfortunately, due to the exodus of players from Nkana, polo ceased to be played there but efforts had been made to encourage farmers in the Mazabuka area to take up the game. The farmers were very enthusiastic and brought their ranch ponies in for practices, and as they improved they began buying thoroughbreds from the race track. The founders of polo in Mazabuka were names such as Bevis Coventry, Charles Stubbs, Dougie Dabbs, Wote Faurie, Dawrie, Dawie Lombard, Cedric Oates and Ewen Pinkney.

Polo tends to be a game that runs in families, and today in Zambia we have the Millers of Lusaka and the Coventry's Stubbs and Kirby's of Mazabuka, with father and sons being able to form some strong teams.

Many teams from various countries have visited Zambia, but polo really improved when Ronnie Ferguson brought out a young Guards team from England. Ronnie Ferguson took time off to coach and instruct the Zambian players in riding and polo tactics. Other teams have come from Kenya,

Ghana, Nigeria, Swaziland, Zimbabwe, Australia, New Zealand and the United States of America. The Zambian side, in turn, has visited Kenya, Ghana, Nigeria Zimbabwe, Lesotho, Swaziland, India, Australia and the United States of America.

In 1985, Zambia hosted a team from Dallas, Texas, led by Buzz Welker and including six goaler Corky Linfoot took hours in explaining to players how to choose ponies, train green ponies, umpire and polo tactics.

The main polo tournaments organized by the Association, apart from internationals against visiting countries, are two or three inter-club tournaments during the polo season which runs from April to September. These tournaments are in two divisions, namely above four goals and below four goals. This system was changed in 1985 and the 'A' league featured teams of eight goals and above, the 'B league two to seven goals and the 'C' league below two goals.

The Zambia Polo Association is affiliated to the Hurlingham Polo Association in England.

International polo returned to Zambia when an American side met in Lusaka in the opening match of their three-game series in Mazabuka. The Americans, led by Buzz Welker, last here in 1981, was a fourteen-goal team and showed some very exciting polo against a Zambian team captained by Paul Taylor.

The Americans who also played Mazabuka had the following handicap:

James Vaughan (1)   Welker (2)   Corky Linfoot (6)
Harley Stimmel (5)

— *Zambia*
Gordon Kirby (3)   Keith Coventry (3)   Paul Taylor (4)
Chris Collett (3)

— *Lusaka*
R. Ranchod (1)   Alf Francis (1)   D. Casilli (1)
Chris Miller (0)

— *Mazabuka*
J. Stubbs (2)   A. Collett (1)   L. Coventry (2)
C. Stubbs (2)

The Americans' tour was their third. The first was in May 1980 and was an eight-goal side for the Caltex Cup. In their first encounter against Lusaka

Polo Club, giving away six and a half goals on handicap, the Americans were unable to make up the deficit and Lusaka won nine and a half to six. Against Zambia B, a six goal team, the Americans displayed that they were settling to their polo though going down by half a goal.

The game against the probable Zambian side was one of the most exciting ever seen in Lusaka, the Americans starting with a two and a half goal handicap lead. Keith Coventry's two goals for Zambia were offset in the last chukka by America's only goal through Ric Warren. The Americans triumphed three and a half to two.

The final clash against Zambia for the Caltex cup, played off scratch, resulted in a very tight, fast and entertaining match. Each team scored two goals in the second chukka. It was not until the fifth chukka that George Alexander scored within the last few moments leaving the Americans three to two victors and deserving winners.

In June 1984 Zambia lost 8-3 to New Zealand in a friendly played in Lusaka. Earlier the Kiwis drew 9-9 with Lusaka Select before defeating Mazabuka Farmers 12-8½.

After playing the Americans, the Zambians faced Kenya. The East Africans ended their tour 4-3 winners against Lusaka Blue. Kenya scored through Gillies Turle (three) and skipper Keith Allen. Ian Miller was Lusaka's three-goal star.

Kenya had beaten Mazabuka Green 3-2 in another tough game. Rick Andersen, Allen and Turle scored for the visitors while Mazabuka scored theirs through George Benda. But the ZPA Blue beat Kenya 5-1. Chris Collett scored three goals and Paul Taylor two. Kenya's only goal came from Andersen.

Impressed with the tour, ZPA Chairman, Alf Francis, said the matches were worthwhile. In the opening matches in Lusaka, ZPA Blue team walloped Kenya 7-2, with Zambia scoring through John Stubbs (three), Mark Harvey (three) and Nittin Patel. ZPA beat Mazabuka Yellow 1-0 and Kenya beat Mazabuka 3-1. Kenya were a seven-goal team which also included Mick Smith.

Tournament Results – 1980

May 2	USA versus Lusaka	6-9½
May3	USA versus Zambia B	2-2½
May 4	USA versus Zambia A	3½-2
May 10	USA versus Mazabuka (Invitation)	8-6
May 11	USA versus Zambia A	3-2
May 30	Kenya versus Lusaka B	10-5½

May 31	Kenya versus Lusaka A	8-6½
June 1	Kenya versus Lusaka B	4-5
June 6	Kenya versus Lusaka Mazabuka Invitation	4-2
June 7	Kenya versus Mazabuka C	6-3
June 8	Kenya versus Zambia	5½-6
June 22	Swaziland versus Lusaka A	8-8½
June 23	Swaziland versus Zambia B	7-5
June 24	Swaziland versus Zambia A	3-8

But behind every chukka of polo there are hours of work and care. The ponies should be as fit as a marathon runner, and it takes a long time to make them ready for each chukka. Then there is the preparation for each day, shearing the manes, bandaging the tails and the firm but gentle bandaging of the legs to protect them against a hit from the ball or stick.

Bridles, saddles and all other tack have to be cleaned and prepared. The ponies have to be loaded on the trucks for the trip to the Polo ground. This takes hours of patience, tenderness and hard work, observed a polo expert, and Polo is here to stay in Zambia.

JUDO

Judo as a sport has gained immense popularity in Zambia.

Professor Jigoro Kano, a great theorist and famous master of Ju-jistu – a violent all-in fighting technique – transformed the art into Judo by removing the violence from it.

In 1882, he established the first Judo school in Tokyo and called it the Kodokan. Today it is looked upon as the cradle of world judo. Judo is a Japanese word – in fact two words JU which means the principle of gentleness and DO meaning the way of gentleness or yielding. Judo is meant to be a way of life.

As the name implies, Judo is a noble sport. There is nothing cruel, painful or violent about real Judo. Young and old people of both sexes can enjoy it. Unlike the majority of sports, Judo has no set seasons and can be enjoyed all year round.

Among the five martial arts, Judo is the Queen – graceful, gentle, beautiful but most effective against violent attack. Judo has nothing to do with fistcuffs or mere brute strength, a popular fallacy associated with martial arts because of Bruce-Lee films. On the contrary, it is an education of the mind and body. It pervades the Judoka's whole life and relationships with people.

An education that develops self-control, alertness, quickness of reaction and perfection of co-ordination, Judo helps to build a truly strong and controlled character. It is worth noting that the medical profession especially recommends Judo for nervous people. It breeds inner security and courage, necessary ingredients for success in facing the battles of life and human existence today.

An important and valuable point is, of course, Judo is also an art of self-defence. Professor Kano said Judo makes real use of mental and bodily energies and shapes a noble character. By regular participation in Judo, a person's ability to co-ordinate mind and body can be fully developed, and very high standards can be reached.

Judo is really a philosophy of life. Ideas, thoughts, reflection, attitude precede action. Actions repeated mould character. All this is not to say that Judo can be picked up or learnt quickly without effort. Like so many other things in life there is only one way to learn, and that is to enter into it in the real spirit, ready to learn all there is to know and a readiness to discipline one's life. Even at seventy years, a master is still learning.

In the second half of the twentieth century, Professor Kano gave Judo to the world as a new sport. Rules were made, throws systematized, holds, locks, strangles were formulated and whole exercise framed in recognized points system. Judo was officially recognized and became an Olympic discipline for the first time at Olympic level in Seoul, Republic of Korea, in 1988.

The contests are held on a special mat (Tatami). The competitors step out on a Tatami in a special uniform (Jodogi), consisting of jackets and trousers. Judo jackets are tied up by a belt. The colour of the belt corresponds with a sportsman's skill and grade. Thus a novice wears a white belt, more experienced Judokas have yellow, orange, violet, blue and brown belts. The master Judokas wear black belts. Dan, master or teacher is the term used for black belt holders. There are ten grades of black belt.

Judo in Zambia

Judo in Zambia appeared with the early pioneers and expatriates who came to work on the mines and elsewhere. Among them were Alec Thompson, Gunter Herman, Len Must, Denis Long, Keith Featherstone, Dave Cummings, Tony Peters, Father Jude McKenna and others. There were clubs on the Copperbelt, Lusaka and Livingstone. In 1970, six Japanese instructors brought in by the Zambia Police brought new life and wider horizons to the sport. Their presence contributed largely to the spread of Judo.

Zambia Police officers were sent to Japan for advanced courses while others went to Britain, Italy and Morocco. Soon Zambians were in the frontline and lifting national titles and gaining places on the international mat. After the basic training and contracts of the first six Japanese Judo experts expired – the Japanese Overseas Co-operation Volunteers (JOVC) sent another four volunteers. They were H. Sasaki, Y. Higashi, O. Okada and Y. Doki who were attached to the various clubs in the country.

In the Lusaka home of Dave Cummings, then Chairman of the Northern Rhodesia Judo Association, the Zambia Judo Association was born. At that meeting all the clubs were represented and the association was affiliated to the National Sports Council of Zambia. Names like Cummings, Father

Jude, Tony Peters, Don King, Bashier Macker, Brian Beharrell, T. Jackson, Roby Oliver, Henry Kaishe, Donald Munakatesho, Paul Luanga and others began to hit the headlines. In the mid 70's and 80's, came David Kayoya, the first Zambian chairman, John Shamboko, first Zambian secretary (after Ken Batchelor had returned to Britain). Spencer Mukubesa, first Zambian treasurer, Paul Luanga, first Zambian coach, Wilson Jumbe and Aggrey Mukanga took turns at chairing the association with Father Jude.

Zambia Judo Association and the International Scene

Zambia's debut in international tournaments came in 1973 when the national team took on Mauritius and Reunion in Livingstone and Lusaka. The Zambian team comprised Cummings, Oliver, Steve Rogerson, Moses Malambo, Amos Hamunyumbwe, Peters, Kaishe, Henry Sichalwe, Munakatesho, George Hamaiko, Kayoya and Father Jude.

Zambia beat the visitors convincingly at both venues. A return match followed with Zambia beating Mauritius 9-0, but losing 5-4 to a powerful team of French Judokas representing Reunion on the Indian Ocean island.

Zambia and Olympic Games

In 1980, the Zambian flag took its honoured place among the great Judo nations of the world when she became a full member of the world and continental bodies governing the sport, namely the International Judo Federation (IJF) and the Africa Judo Union (AJU). She 'came of age' at the 22nd Moscow Olympics in the Soviet Union.

It was an initiation ceremony and a 'baptism of fire' never to be forgotten. Zambian Judokas fought with world champions and the best men from Czechoslovakia, Belgium, Hungary, Cuba, Britain, Syria, Australia and Cameroun. The six Zambian representatives were: Charles Chibwe (Livingstone), Francis Mwanza (Chipata), George Hamaiko (Livingstone), Henry Sichalwe (Livingstone), Donald Munakatesho (Mongu) and Rex Chizooma (Kamfinsa). Father Jude was the coach and Aggrey Mukanga chairman.

To prepare for the Olympics, Zambia met Zimbabwe in Harare. Zambia met Czechoslovakia in Ostrava and lost 4-2. It was a last hour 'warm-up' before Moscow and an indication of things to come. At the Olympics, Chizooma lost to World and Olympic Champion Robert van de Walla of Belgium, Munakatesho lost to Isaac Azcuy (Cuba), Sichalwe lost to Vladimir Barta (Czechoslovakia), Hamaiko lost to Maurice Nkamdem (Cameroun), Mwanza lost to Michael Young (Australia) and Chibwe lost to Squir Elnajaar

(Syria). 'The experience gained, however, far outweighed all the gold, silver and bronze medals in Moscow,' said Father Jude.

After Moscow, the sky was the limit for Zambia. Zimbabwe was invited for a return match on 6 June 1981 at Nakatindi Hall in Lusaka, and this time the two teams drew.

In February 1982, the Japanese Embassy brought four Judo experts from Nippon Budokan (Japan Martial Arts Centre), two world champions among them, who staged demonstrations in the latest Judo techniques. At the grading session which followed four judokas Father Jude, Luanga, Munakatesho and Malambo received third Dan.

Later a ten-man Zambian team was sent to Cairo, Egypt, for a debut in the All-Africa Championships. The squad consisted of Aggrey Mukanga, Father Jude (team manager), Luanga (coach), Kaishe, James Ngoma, Alick Kalwizhi, Asaph Tembo, Wilson Jumbe, Chizooma and Sichalwe. Zambia finished fourteenth out of the twenty-three countries represented.

The third encounter with Zimbabwe was held on 19 September, 1982 at Alexander Club in Harare. Zambia was in an uncompromising mood, beating the hosts 9-4. Three Zambians: Jerome Mwalongo, Chiwale Choopa and Alfred Daka won by 'knockouts' or full points. At a re-match in Livingstone, Zambia hammered Zimbabwe 10-3.

A Superstar is Buried

The most tragic event in Judo circles was the death of a prominent judoka Charles Chibwe (twenty-one years), on 2 April, 1983. The sensational Chibwe had represented Zambia at many international tournaments, including the 1980 Moscow Olympics, and was the national champion in his weight category. Chibwe died when the car in which he was a passenger plunged into the Zambezi river in Livingstone. It was Good Friday but a bad day for Zambian Judo.

In 1983, Father Jude led a team to the All-Africa Championships which were held in Dakar, Senegal. The team managed by John Shamboko, coached by Luanga with fighters Kaishe, Sichalwe, Asaph Tembo and Felix Kalumba, returned home empty-handed. It was a tour marred by many problems in transportation and accommodation.

Zambia at World Championships

The year 1983 will be remembered when the youth team of Patrick Mali, Felix Kalumba, Stephen Manda and Nyambe Yamboto participated in the World Youth Championships in Mayaguez, Puerto Rico. Making their debut, Zambia came out eleventh out of the twenty-three countries.

During the same year three judokas received International Judo Federation (IJF) coaching certificates after attending a course in Moscow. They were: Father Jude, Luanga and Spencer Mukubesa, who was the first Zambian to walk on a world championship Tatami.

The tour of Kenya in June 1984 to prepare for the Los Angeles Olympics was the most successful international outing ever. The team with regular faces comprised leader Father Jude, Shamboko (manager), coach Luanga, James Mafuta, Kalwizhi, Tembo and Sichalwe. The final score was seventeen points for Zambia and three for Kenya. Mafuta became the youngest Zambian Judoka to be awarded a black belt at the age of sixteen.

He was awarded the black belt by Dr. D. S. Kim, seventh dan black belt holder and Kenya national coach. The first three best Zambian Judokas of the tour went on to represent Zambia in the Los Angeles Olympics. Sichalwe was dropped for want of places.

The first East and Central African Championships in Lusaka in 1985 saw Zambia lift six of the eight gold medals. This was Zambia's most glorious hour. The gold medallists coached by Luanga were: Hebert Pumulo, Mafuta, Griffiths Ngongolo, Kalwizhi, Kenneth Imwinji and Chizooma. Zimbabwe lifted two gold medals and Kenya came third. The tournament was sponsored by the Harrington Brothers of Senanga and Livingstone.

The Casablanca All-Africa Championships in Morocco in 1986 saw Zambia emerged in fourth place behind Algeria, Morocco, Tunisia and Egypt. Father Jude McKenna was elected vice-president of the African Judo Union (AJU). Business houses are taking keen interest in sponsoring ZJA to achieve its aims towards the development of the sport.

Judo would not have gained prominence in Zambia today without Father Jude McKenna who, known as Father Judo and Father Zambian Judo, in most cases managed to find sponsors to finance trips to various tournaments outside the country. Others who have done a lot for judo in the country are Luanga (coach), J.R. Nayee of Livingstone, the Harrington Brothers and Ken Bachelor, who retired as ZJA secretary in 1981, and was replaced by Shamboko and Ricky Kauta. 'Judo in Zambia is becoming more and more popular. The introduction of Judo in schools will go a long way in increasing its popularity, national coach Luanga, said. At least one or two clubs are affiliated to the ZJA. One generous and practical donor to the ZJA has been Fred Mwala of Mongu who once gave a cow to the national team.

The ZJA has clubs at Livingstone – police and Zambia Air Force (Red Arrows), Lusaka Central Sports, Ndola, Mongu Police, St. John's Secondary School (Mongu), Holy Cross Secondary School (Mongu), Malengwa (Mongu), Mongu Teachers Training College, ZAF (Lusaka), Zambia Army

(Lusaka), Zambia National Service (Lusaka), Chipata Police and Paramilitary (Lilayi).

The fourth All-Africa Games story began on 11 July 1987 when seven fighting men emerged to take their place with the Zambia Olympic, Commonwealth and All-Africa Games Association (ZOCAGA's) best in Kenya. The judokas were Herbert Pumulo, Mafuta, Ngongolo, Kalwizhi, Boniface Mbewe, Sichalwe and Chizooma.

60 Kg Hebert Pumulo: (Green Buffaloes). National Champion 1987 ECA gold medal winner and Championship title. Represented Zambia in Casablanca African Championships in 1986. Top judoka in Zambia in 1986.

65 Kg James Mafuta: (Zambia National Service). National Champion 1987. ECA gold medal winner and championship title. Represented Zambia at the last two continental Championships and also in Los Angeles Olympics.

71 Kg Griffiths Ngongolo: (Red Arrows). Champion 1987 ECA gold medal winner and championship title. Represented Zambia at two Africa Championships in Tunisia and Morocco where his performance won him the title of 'our top performance.'

78 Kg Alick Kalwizhi: (Red Arrows). Champion 1987, ECA gold and championship title. Represented Zambia many times, at 4th Africa Championships Cairo, Tunis, Dakar, Casablanca and at the Los Angeles Olympics

86 Kg Boniface Mbewe: (Green Buffaloes). National Champion 1987. Represented Zambia in Casablanca Africa Championships. Captain of the Army team.

95 Kg Henry Sichalwe: (Red Arrows). Longest serving international in the team. Champion 1987. Fought for Zambia in the Moscow Olympics. Travelled to more than 15 countries in contests. International referee – but now making 'come-back' to the continental scene where he previously represented Zambia in Cairo, Dakar and Rabat.

95 Kg Rex Chizooma: (Zambia Police). Heavyweight Champion 1987. Open Champion 1987. Weight 105 Kg. ECA gold medalist and champion. Represented Zambia in Cairo and at Moscow Olympics.

Inspector Paul Luanga: National coach for seven years. Position which he took over from Father Jude after the Moscow Olympics. National Champion. International 3rd Dan black belt holder. Course persued in Japan, Holland and Russia. Took national team to Egypt. Led team to Kenya, United Kingdom, Zaire (now the Democratic Republic of the Congo), Mauritius, Reunion, USA, Russia, Morocco, Senegal, Zimbabwe, Tunisia and Puerto Rico.

TABLE TENNIS

The Zambia Table Tennis Association (ZTTA) was formed in 1970 at a meeting held at the Raylton Club in Ndola after the Zambia Closed tournament. The tournament was won by Chingola's Brian Ryan after having beaten Samuel Kasama in the quarter finals and Roger Gill in the semi-finals. The following were elected:

Abdul Dudhia (Lotus, Lusaka) – Chairman
Vitor Mwandila (ZAF, Lusaka) – Vice-Chairman
Duncan Moseley (Ndola) – Secretary
Tony Kosoko (Mufulira) – Treasurer

The ZTTA became an affiliate of the National Sports Council of Zambia in 1973.

Prior to the formation of the ZTTA, there existed two separate associations – the Copperbelt Table Tennis Association, which was in existence as early as 1967, and the Midlands Table Tennis Association. Players from Lusaka and Kabwe took part in tournaments on the Copperbelt, such as the Copperbelt Open, the Zambia Closed and the Zambia Open.

Duncan Moseley was more instrumental in putting table tennis on the Zambian map. He was also responsible for introducing the game to indigenous Zambians by paying frequent visits to places like Mufulira, Chingola and Kabwe to begin with and then spreading to Kitwe, Luanshya and Lusaka. In this endeavour he received considerable support from the likes of fellow expatriates such as Hollies, Roger Gill, Henegan, Oscar Quadros, Brian Ryan, Cardoso and Zukas, to name but a few.

1970 saw the first indigenous Zambians elected to the Ndola Board. These were Samuel Kasama (Vice –Chairman) and Bongo Mwale (Committee

Member). The first and second indigenous Zambian chairmen were Bongo Mwale and Pygnar Msiska respectively. They too contributed considerably to the game as witnessed by the buying of fuel from personal funds by Msiska to ferry players to various locations to participate in tournaments. Albert Bwalya was the first indigenous general secretary of the Association and between 1973-1974 also contributed considerably to the administration of the game, culminating in a trip to China by a Zambian team.

Other administrators worth mentioning were Joel Bwalya, vice-chairman from 1977-1979; Misheck Sondashi, general secretary from 1975-1979; Bentley Mumba, treasurer from 1972-1974; Peter Kalumbe, treasurer from 1974-1976; Sean Gallagher for the inauguration of Junior table tennis clubs in Luanshya in 1976; Ragnar Aasen who was responsible for the improvement of standards in Lusaka and the formation of the Midlands League in conjunction with Samuel Kasama of Kabwe. Aasen also takes credit on behalf of the ZTTA for the negotiations with a Lusaka firm to manufacture table tennis tables.

During a dull spell in the game between 1978-79, a team headed by Charles Chenda and comprising the likes of Sheck Kambafwile, organizing secretary; Samuel Kasama, general secretary; Philip Jere, vice-chairman and National Coach and Peter Chanda, worked tirelessly to get the game back on top.

Clive Pitts, a great champion between 1971-74, introduced the 'spin' shot to the Zambian game. The 'loop,' adopted during the trip to China, was introduced to the Zambian game by Bongo Mwale. The combination of both shots turned Samuel Kasama into a first class player from 1973-79 and also resulted in the improvement of standards to the game. Mathews Sikanyika, perhaps the best defensive player Zambia has ever seen, trained a number of budding players in Mufulira.

Roger Gill, Brian Ryan, Oscar Quadros, Clive Pitts, Peter Godfrey, Philip Crane, Harry Gaunt, Bongo Mwale, Samuel Kasama, Benson Mwape, Shailesh Patel, Evaristo Kamayamba, Biggy Banda, Boyd Kabinda, Kennedy Chaonsa, Webbyster Mulopa, Mathews Sikanyika, Henry Chibulu, Edwin Sisya, Julius Kunda, Vincent Nkole and Erasmus Masuwa were all at one time or another listed as champions in one or more of the following tournaments:

Zambia Open	Zambia Closed
Copperbelt Open	Copperbelt Closed
Midlands Open	Midlands Closed
Kalulushi Open	Ndola Open
Nchanga Open	Lusaka Open

The ZTTA participated in various notable championships as follows:

1971
(a)   *Kenya Tour of Zambia*
       Contingent: 6 (including reserves)
       Consisting of Clive Pitts, Harry Gaunt, Oscar Quadros, Bongo
       Mwale, Bwalya of Chingola and Samuel Kasama.
       Drew 5-5 in Lusaka, lost 0-5 in Ndola and 2-5 in Chingola.

(b)   *Zambia Tour of China*
       Contingent: 4
       The team consisted of Bongo Mwale, Prabhat Vashi, Gershom
       Mwansa and Victor Mwandila.
       The Zambians played against world class players and were all
       beaten in the preliminaries.

1973: Asian, African and Latin American Games – Beijing, China
       Contingent 4
       The team consisted of Bongo Mwale, Victor Mwandila, Collins
       Sapallo, Bentley Mumba, Samuel Kasama and Mathews
       Sikanyika, and lost in the preliminary rounds in both the singles
       and team events. However, playing in the doubles, the team of
       Mathews Sikanyika and Samuel Kasama managed to reach the
       second round.

1975: *Asian, African and Latin American Games – Lagos, Nigeria*
         Contingent 2
         These consisted of Bongo Mwale and Samuel Kasama. Kasama
         was rated 98th out of a total of 1,200 players. This represents the
         highest rating achievement by a Zambian table tennis player.

1976: Kasama nominated to the Organising Committee of the Asian,
African and Latin American Games held in Mexico City. At the same Games
the third coaching seminar was conducted by the Chinese, the other two
having been conducted in Peking (now Beijing) and Lagos.

1977:
(a)   Bongo Mwale attended a coaching Clinic in Alexandria, Egypt, and
       was awarded a certificate with merit.

(b)　　*Zambian Tour of Tanzania*
　　　　Contingent: 5
　　　　These consisted of Pygnar Msiska (Team Leader), Bongo Mwale, Ben Mwape, Prabhat Vashi and Ellias Jere. The team lost all their games.

1981:
(a)　　*Colgate Palmolive Open – Lusaka Zambia*
　　　　Zimbabwe were invited to participate and won all the events.

(b)　　*Tanzania Tour of Zambia*
　　　　Contingent: 5
　　　　Coaches: Mathews Sikanyika and Samuel Kasama
　　　　The team consisted of Evariso Kamayamba, Biggy Banda, Webbyster Mulopa, Lennox Changala and Vincent Nkole.
　　　　Tanzania won the first game 5-2, the second 5-4 and lost the third 2-5 proving that the Tanzanian standard of play was far superior to that of the Zambians.

(c)　　*Zambia Tour of Zimbabwe*
　　　　Contingent: 5
　　　　Zambia won the junior singles events. Mathews Sikanyika and Samuel Kasama played the duel roles of players/coaches.

1983:　*Mozambique Tour of Zambia and Colgate Palmolive Open*
　　　　Mozambique lost to Zambia in the team events, but one of their players won the Colgate Palmolive Open.

1984: Colgate Palmolive Open
　　　　Angola were invited to participate in this tournament, but lost all their games.

　　　　The deaths of Albert Bwalya, who was the first Zambian general secretary, and Cardoso, who was responsible for the Luanshya clubs in the Ndola/Luanshya League, robbed the game of dedicated players and administrator.
　　　　The highlights of the game could be listed as Evaristo Kamayamba winning the Zimbabwe Junior Championships in Harare in 1981, the sponsoring of the Copperbelt Open in Ndola by Reckitt and Coleman in 1985 and Zambia beating Tanzania 5-2 at the Raylton Club in the same year, 1985. It was an action packed year which also saw women taking active part in the game.

The future of the game in Zambia could be said to be promising as a result of many more clubs on the Copperbelt and the Midlands participating, but there is still the worry of the shortage of administrators as most players tend to lose interest after leaving school or the university thus creating a vacuum, coupled with the shortage and exhorbitant price of equipment. One would also like to see the game further popularized in the rural areas of the country.

LAWN TENNIS

Soon after independence, lawn tennis was an expatriate dominated sport. Indigenous Zambians were playing tennis but neither league nor competitive tennis. The ruling bodies were entirely non-Zambian. Towards the mid-sixties coaching classes for juniors were started at the Lusaka Club by Ian Nichols and Solly Patel and amongst their students were Dick Mpheneka, Waza Kaunda and Douglas Meleki.

Towards the end of the sixties and early seventies more Zambians took up the sport and started playing at competitive levels. Amongst the few Zambians at this level were Godwin Mumba, Billy Mulenga and Andrew Zengeni, to name but a few. The first Zambians to represent the Midlands in the annual Midlands versus Copperbelt match were Maxwell Sichula and Billy Mulenga.

The mid-seventies saw an upsurge in both the playing and the administration of tennis. The Midlands Lawn Tennis Association was headed by Lt. General Benjamin Mibenge and the Zambia Lawn Tennis Association by Maxwell Sichula (since 1973).

The first Zambian tennis team which played against Mauritius in 1975 was headed by Maxwell Sichula and the team members included Tina Ship, Ian Nichols, Solly Patel, Norma Jamieson, Clive Ross, amongst others (non-Zambians). A look at the annual rankings for the year 1974 compared to the ranking list for 1978 will indicate the change that took place and the steady and rapid ascendancy of Zambian players at national level.

Dick Mpheneka was the first indigenous Zambian to win a major title when he won the Midlands Open Singles against Egil Stokke in 1978. Whereas in the early seventies the household names in tennis were Ian Sharp, Warwick Chapman, Chris Nell and Norma Jamieson (Copperbelt), Ian Nichols, Solly Patel, Tina Ship and Bjorn Lunoe (Midlands), towards the end of the seventies it was Dick Mpheneka, Mambo Njovu, Fred Kangwa and Douglas Mumba.

Today's leading players are all Zambian and the standard of tennis is higher than after Zambia's political independence. A coaches association has also been formed for promoting tennis amongst juniors and has held courses to train local coaches. The courses were conducted by Solly Patel, who is a qualified professional coach.

At the administration level, the Zambia Lawn Tennis Association is practically all Zambian and so are the local associations. All the recent Zambian teams have been fully Zambian having been selected purely on merit. The top players today include Patrick Kangwa, Mambo Njovu, Dick Mpheneka and David Mutale. Kela Simunyola and Steven Kangwa are studying in the United States on tennis scholarships. Fred Kangwa is playing on the professional tennis circuit in Europe and America.

There are a number of achievements Zambia has scored in the sport of Lawn Tennis since October, 1964. Below are some of the major ones:

(a) The organization and administration of the sport is firmly in the hands of Zambians at clubs, regional and national levels. This is important for a number of reasons. Firstly, it provides for continuity. Expatriates come and go and although they can and have contributed greatly to the development of the sport, one cannot always guarantee they will be around to see agreed development plans through.

Secondly, the localization of administration of the sport ought to ensure that the sport is given proper cultural and political orientation as it develops.

(b) The second most important achievement is the encouragement given to junior tennis in the last ten years or so as reflected in regional and national programmes today.

Juniors compete in four age-groups – under 12, 14, 16 and 18 – in the Midlands and Copperbelt regional tournaments. The same applies in national junior tournaments. Since 1985, an international junior tournament sponsored by Colgate Palmolive (Zambia) was introduced and prooved to be very competitive with several African countries taking part. The participation of young Zambians of tender age in tennis is an investment in the future of sport. The achievements of one time junior tennis players like Steven Kangwa and Kela Simunyola now in the United States of America not only encourage other youngsters to follow their footsteps but guarantees the future's long-term development of the sport.

Some of the prominent champions that come to mind from about 1967 are:

Men	Women
Peter Abe	Norma Jamieson
Arichandran	Jenny Howard
Cecil Jacobs	Tina Ship
Clive Ross	Veronica Zulu (now Mrs Mpheneka)
Alan King	Nora Maibwe
Egil Stokke	Diedre Dunphy
Dick Mpheneka	
Hudak	
Fred Kangwa	
Mambo Njovu	
Patrick Kangwa	

Several people have been instrumental in bringing the game of tennis to its present level. The following come to mind:

—— *Norma Jamieson*

She was for many years women's champion and also a part-time coach at her club in Chingola. For many years Jamieson was an official on both the Copperbelt Board later changed to Copperbelt Lawn Tennis Association and the Zambia Lawn Tennis Association.

—— *Godwin Mumba*

He was one of the first few Zambians to play competitive tennis and became the first indigenous Vice-Chairman of the Zambia Lawn Tennis Association. Among other things he was instrumental in introducing the Zambian Open in 1972.

—— *Solly Patel*

Player, administrator and coach. He has devoted a great deal of his spare time to tennis organization at various levels in different capacities for many years.

— *Maxwell Sichula*

Was the first indigenous Chairman of the Zambia Lawn Tennis Association from 1973 to 1982. He was one of the top Zambian players in the country. Born in Chingola in 1938. He started his tennis as a ball boy before he moved to Munali Secondary School in Lusaka where he captained the school team. When he left school he went to Kabwe where he formed a tennis club. He then went to Canada and was a member of the Manitoba University team. He was also a member of the Winnipeg Tennis Club. He returned to Mufulira where he was Club's singles and doubles champion in 1971.

Sichula was one of the founder members of Kantanshi Tennis Club which, under his guidance, became a tennis force to be reckoned with. He is currently a member of Lusaka Tennis Club and former National Sports Council of Zambia Chairman.

— *Ian Nichols*

A ranked player both in the singles and doubles for many years, Nichols was a good tennis administrator and played various roles in the administration of tennis in Zambia. Easily one of the most committed administrators during his time. He was born in Melbourne, Australia. He started tennis at the age of eight. Before coming to Zambia (he has since left) in 1964, he played the Victorian Country Tennis Circuit for Dunlop. Among his successes whilst in Zambia were being champion of the Midlands Men's Doubles from 1965 to 1972, except for 1966 and Midlands Men's Singles and Mixed Doubles Champion in 1971 and 1972. With Jokinnen, he was Zambian Men's Doubles Champion in 1969 and 1970. In 1970 with the same partner, he reached the quarter finals of the Kenya Open. He toured Mauritius with the 1973 Midlands side. He worked for a local construction company in Lusaka.

— *K. Arichandran*

'Ari' as he was known to all the Zambian tennis fraternity, arrived in Zambia in December 1971 and was a member of the Ndola Lawn Tennis Club. He was Zambian and Copperbelt Men's and Mixed Doubles Champion. He was born in Colombo, Sri Lanka, in June 1932. He started tennis at the age of sixteen and was Captain of the Sri Lanka University team.

— *Renee Bailey*

Renee was born in Kimberly, South Africa, where she started tennis at the age of ten. At fifteen she won her first major tournament – the Border Championships. She was South African non-White Women's Singles champion for eleven years before coming to Zambia in 1966. While in Zambia she played in the National Women's finals. She was Women's Doubles Champion and played in many Copperbelt finals.

── *Ralph Bailey*

Ralph Bailey was born in Cape Town, South Africa, in 1933 and was married to Renee Bailey. He started tennis very late at the age of twenty-one. Since arriving in Zambia, both Ralph and Renee were regular members of the Copperbelt team and played for Roan Tennis Club. They were both triple champions every year.

── *Peter Abe*

Abe was born in Ober Hause, Germany, in 1940. He started tennis at the age of thirteen in 1953. He won his first tournament at the age of fourteen, which was the Junior club Championships in Hamm. At the age of fifteen he won the town championship. In 1961, he was a winner of the 'B' Tournament in Wesphalia. In February, 1967, he came to Zambia and joined Rhokana Tennis Club. He won the Zambian Men's singles in 1970 as well as the Men's Doubles. With his partner, Chris Nell, Abe was Copperbelt Men's Doubles champion many times. He was a regular member of the Copperbelt team since arriving in Zambia.

── *Cecil Jacobs*

Jacobs was born in Kimberly, South Africa. He started tennis at the age of sixteen and although it was only his fourth sport, he liked cricket as well.

Like most sports in Zambia, the lack of adequate resources like equipment and finance, especially during the years when Zambia experienced serious economic problems was a major constraint to the promotion and development of tennis.

All the required tennis equipment has to be imported as there are no facilities within the country, at the moment, to make it. Foreign exchange is therefore necessary but because this has not been easily available, the shortage and lack of some equipment has been quite serious. Where the equipment has been imported into the country, the cost to the average tennis player has been very high and out of reach to most.

The other problem constraining the development and improvement of standards of the game is the inadequate coaching facilities. There are very few qualified coaches in the country and nearly all of them qualified to teach beginners only.

In the last few years, many juniors have taken up the game of tennis. A good number of these have reached a standard of play requiring the services of a qualified coach to lift the game further.

If the Zambian Lawn Tennis Association had sufficient funds at its disposal, the problem of lack of good coaches would be overcome somewhat by sending some of the more promising young tennis players to compete and receive coaching lessons outside the country.

Tennis has definitely improved since independence. Were it not for the constraints, some of which have been listed earlier, one could argue and quite rightly too, that the game would have improved, even more than it has.

Today, not only have the standards improved, but the majority of the top players are indigenous Zambians.

In the region, Zambia is probably the second strongest country in tennis after Zimbabwe.

The future of tennis in Zambia is bright, given efficient administration of the sport. The talent is there in abundance but, like in other sport, this needs to be developed through proper and regular coaching backed by regular local and international competitions.

Figure 20: The Kangwa brothers: Fred (middle) was the
first to leave for the United States of America. The players
were household names in lawn tennis in Zambia.

Figure 21: Lawn tennis has come a long way, thanks
to the Zambia Tennis Association.

SQUASH

Squash was introduced to Zambia (Northern Rhodesia) by the early settlers who had picked up the skills and love for it from their days of service during the Second World War. The building of courts was usually spearheaded by such people. Livingstone had a squash court as early as 1940, Mazabuka in 1946, Mbala in 1947 and Kabwe in 1948. Such courts were part of the settlement's recreation centres.

In the mining towns the mining companies themselves erected squash courts as part of the social amenities for the use by their employees. Until the mid- 1960's squash was regarded as an expatriate social sport and the playing of the game was confined to the expatriate community.

In 1958 a Squash Association was formed, mainly to co-ordinate inter club competitions run between Copperbelt towns. The Association did not stage any tournaments of its own until 1960 when the Northern Rhodesia Championship proper was held.

The formation of a National Association led to increased exposure of the game to Zambian players through participation in regional and friendly test matches against Kenya, Malawi, Tanzania and Zimbabwe.

Shortly after independence the Zambia Squash Rackets Association, in a bid to increase participation and improve standards, approached various airlines to sponsor air tickets to enable the Association bring in touring teams as well as invite overseas players to participate in the two major tournaments – the Copperbelt Open and the Zambia Open. Until the late 1970's the major supporters of these tournaments were British Airways and BOAC (British Overseas Airways Corporation).

The boom in indigenous Zambian participation in the game of squash came in the early 1970's, mainly after being exposed to lawn tennis. By the mid-1970's Zambia could boast of a handful of good indigenous Zambian players such as Mark Banda of Nchanga, Clement Mulenga of Ndola, Willie Kapwasha of Lusaka, Jack Mutale of Ndola and Fred Silungwe of Kabwe. Howeever, the game continued to be dominated by expatriate players such as Joyce Maycock, Jenny Parker and Maggie Masson in the women's section, and by Lusaka's Storr Hunter, Harry O'Connor, Barry Dunphy, Davy Coy, Chibuluma's Peter Charge and Paeder MacGowan of Luanshya.

In 1976 Harry O'Connor of Lusaka Club won the Zambian Veterans' tournament and was sponsored the following year to participate in the World Veterans' Championship held in Canada. O'Connor won the tournament that year, thus bringing Zambia its first taste of international glory.

In the early eighties, thanks largely to the efforts of Liam Sweeney of Chibuluma and Paeder McGowan of Luanshya, young Zambians began to emerge on the squash scene, mainly on the Copperbelt. The Zambia Closed which for years was the preserve of Dinesh Patel and Peter Charge of Chibuluma suddenly began to be threatened by a new squash star Philip Musonda. Musonda, a progeny of Sweeney first hit the limelight with Zambian badminton star Simon Gondwe nipping eagerly at his heels.

Along with them came a host of other Zambians showing that the flood-gate for indigenous squash had now been truly opened. Players like Caeser Kayange, Nick Champo, Harry Sungula, Saliman Quadri, Harry Johnson and Charles Ferreira steadily improved their games and regularly made up the quarter and semi-finalist at each major tournament.

On a team basis too, Zambia gradually began to emerge as a strong contender for the zonal championship. In the East and Central Africa championship, both the Zambia the Zambian women's and men's teams struggled unsuccessfully against Kenya and Zimbabwe, having till 1985 to settle for third position. While the teams vied unsuccessfully for the regional championships, individual players scored greater success. Simon Gondwe won the Mauritius Open in 1984, Phillip Musonda, the Botswana Open and Kenya Open in 1985, and Gavin Apple, the Zambia Junior Open in 1985. In the women's event Jenny Parker and Hilda Edwards also scored personal successes by twice reaching the finals of the individual events of the Central African Championships.

On the women's Squash scene, the departure of Joyce Maycock from Zambia in the 80's led to a see-saw battle between Maggie Masson of Nkana and Jenny Parker of Lusaka. Under Parker's tutelage Hilda Edwards began to emerge as a major figure on the Midlands scene while the Copperbelt saw Judith Chola and Recreena Banda rise to the forefront.

On the management scene too, expatriate management was slow to give way to Zambianisation. In the three major clubs, Ndola, Kitwe and Lusaka chairmanship remained in expatriate hands.

In Lusaka for instance Newton Musanya became the first Zambian Chairman when Atiq Rahman stepped down in 1985. In 1985, the National Association saw the first Zambian chairman in Mike Kabwe leading an almost indigenous executive committee with Rahman being the only exception in the main body.

Development of Squash in Zambia in 1980's

New ZSRA secretary Fidelis Kayula said development of squash among indigenous Zambians has been noticed during the eighties (from 1980 up to date).

That was due to two main factors: Administration. ZSRA became fully Zambianised from 1984 after the election of Mike Kabwe as chairman, and Newton Musanya (secretary). Kabwe served the association for two terms of office (4 years) until October 1987, when the committee led by Brigadier General Musho Moono, chairman and Kayula as secretary took over and; involvement of BP Zambia Ltd in squash promotion with the commencement of BP invitation tournament for indigenous Zambians only in 1980.

ZSRA – Squash development

Since 1984 ZSRA made a decision that only Zambians should represent the country in continental tournaments. Thus the association embarked on Squash promotion among the youth, which saw the emergence of talented squash players such as Phillip Musonda, Simon Gondwe and Jeff Silungwe.

This youthful group formed a team which won the East and Central African Squash tournament of 1986 in Malawi and 1987 in Zimbabwe. In 1985 Musonda won both the Botswana Open and Kenya Open with Gondwe as runner-up

In 1987 Musonda won the individual tournament of East and Central African championship in Lusaka beating Gondwe. To-date Musonda and Gondwe are ranked on the East and Central African Championship level, which is a very big development of squash for the country. Musonda and Gondwe had coaching stints in Britain.

In Squash, women have dominated the Rothmans of Pall Mall (Zambia) sponsored Sportswoman of the year award winning it five times through Joyce Maycock (1978 and 1979), Jenny Parker (1983) and Hilda Edwards (1984 and 1986).

The record is only equaled by athletes who won the award in 1971 (Audrey Chikani), 1972 (Grace Munene), 1976 (Carol Mumbi) 1985 (Litah Muluka) and 1987 (Martha Lungu).

Lusaka Squash Club chairman, Atiq Rahman, said squash has grown in popularity as evidenced by the increase in the number indigenous players in his club alone from 30 in 1981 to over 200 in 1987.

The year 1980 is also worth mentioning, for Jenny Parker who was in Joyce Maycock's shadow was runners-up for the Rothmans of Pall Mall sportswoman of the year award.

Parker's victories included the Zambia Closed, Midlands Open and Copperbelt Open. She was also in the national team that played against Nigeria and Kenya.

Some Notable results in 1980

— *Zambia Open – Lusaka*
Men's event: Fathim Gul of Pakistan beat Shan Zaman (Pakistan) 3-0

Men's Plate: Brian Woods (Zambia) beat Clive Sinclair (UK) 3-0

Women's event: Joyce Maycock beat Faith Sinclair (UK) 3-0

Women's Plate: Hilda Edwards (nee Simbayi) beat Marion Richardson 3-2

— *Lusaka Club Championships*
Men's event: Clement Mulenga beat Ali Malik 3-2

Men's Plate: Alex Machamanda beat Mike Barret 3-0

Women's event: Jenny Parker beat Tricia Dickenson 3-0

Women's Plate: Maggie Langston beat Marion Richardson 3-2

— *British Caledonian-Dunlop Squash Classic – Lusaka 1981*
   Peter Charge 3 Dinesh Patel 2

Plate Competition: Lars Andersen 3 Trevor Parker 0

— *Kenya Cup – Chingola*
Main event: Luanshya beat Nchanga 4-1

Plate event: Lusaka 5 Kabwe 0

— *Midlands Open – Kabwe*
Men's competition: Colin Belshaw beat Paedar MacGowan 3-1

Men's Plate: Lars Andersen beat Crawford Masson 3-0

Women's event: Jenny Parker beat Penny Sutton 3-0

Women's Plate: Heather Balshaw beat Carol Woods 3-1

— *Copperbelt Open – Ndola*
Men's event: Neil Harvey (UK) beat Paul Wright (UK) 3-0

Men's Plate: Fanwell Mutukwa beat H. Mwenechanya 3-1

Women's event: Maggie Masson beat Jenny Parker 3-0

Women's Plate: Rose Sanderson beat Karen Parker 3-0

— *ECA Championship – Kenya 1985*
Zambia finished second to Kenya in the women's individual and team events
and won the men's and women's plate Championships.

— *Zambia Closed – Lusaka*
Phillip Musonda retained the men's singles title after beating Simon Gondwe
9-2, 5-9, 9-4, 9-3 in the final.

Jenny Parker beat Hilda Edwards 9-5, 6-9, 9-3, 9-0 to retain the crown.

— *Kenya Open – Nairobi*
Phillip Musonda was crowned Kenya Open Men's singles champion when he
beat Gondwe 3-1 in the final.

Figure 22: Squash queen, Victoria Chishimba, dominated in Zambia.

BOWLS

The African sun ablaze in an azure firmament; Artic wintry winds driving boiling clouds across a mackerel sky with the promise of a tropical deluge; a balmy breeze to bathe the sweated brow; it makes no difference to that ancient breed called bowlers performed their weekly rituals, said an expert.

The clanging bell summons all to silence when, with solemn dignity the official scorecards, enscribed with names of adversaries and the rink whereon they vie for honours, are announced and distributed to the teams who stoically wend their various ways towards that verdant piece of pasture called the green. Thus another match, competition or tournament in the game of bowls begins.

To the uninitiated, the game of bowls it is believed has its origin buried in medieval England, probably devised by a humble monk of an ancient illustrious order. The game certainly goes back to the thirteenth century and, in its earlier day, its popularity was such that it was one of the games officially legislated against as likely to attract people away from archery.

In the seventeenth century bowls fell on evil times as many greens were attached to taverns and the game acquired the reputation of being merely an adjunct to pothouse revelry. However, it was in Scotland that the game was resurrected to its ethereal level, never again to sink so near to oblivion.

Bowls as played today, is actually two separate games, each with its own supporters and a few players of one attempting the other. These are the Rink or Level Green game and the Crown Green game. As the names imply, it is the nature of the green rather than the objectives of the games that is different and it is the former which is played in Zambia.

The game is played on a perfectly level piece of well-cared-for turf approximately forty metres square divided into strips six metres wide called rinks, the whole-being surrounded by a shallow ditch and low bank. The rinks are delineated by light string being stretched tightly along the surface of the turf and it is within this prescribed area that individual games are played. The game is played between sides of one, two, three or four players. The major game is the Fours in which a team consists of a Lead, a Second, a Third and a Skip, depending on the order in which they play.

The basic equipment of the game is a jack, bowls and a mat. The jack is a small white round ball made of composite material about sixty millimeters in diameter, weighing some twenty-five grams. The bowl is an almost spherical brown or black ball made up of similar material, one hundred and twenty millimeters in diameter and weighing up to 1.59 kilogrammes. The mat on which the players stand whilst delivering their bows, is 14 inches wide and 24 inches long.

The object of the game is to deliver the bowl, which has a bias, so that it runs smoothly up to the green and curves gently onto the jack which has been previously delivered by the first to play. Each team play alternately and in turn and when all bowls have come to rest the team which has bowls nearer the jack than the nearest of their opponents' scores that number of shots. The playing of the jack and all the bowls of all the players in one direction is called an 'end.' The winner is the team accumulating most shots over twenty-one ends or within a certain present time limit.

Each player in each end delivers four bowls when playing Singles or Pairs, three bowls in Triples or two bowls in a Fours game. The distance between the mat and the jack varying between twenty-two to thirty-six metres, the length of the grass (the speed of the green), the variances in wind strength and the dampness of the green make proficiency in the game a very skillful art requiring dedication, concentration and many hours of consistent practice to perfect.

The mythical days of the 'old man's game' are dead and gone as the exuberance of youth has brought an aggressive element into the game. Instead of gently stroking the bowl up the green, players with very little hope of 'drawing' to the jack, will hurl their bow at great speed (fire) to force their opponents' bowls away from the jack or to move the jack to a position more advantageous to their team. This delivery is fraught with dangers as one is just likely to improve the opponents' position.

No great degree of strength is required to play the game which is enjoyed by both sexes in many countries throughout the world. Indeed, age offers barriers as there are many teenage world champions in the making and there are several 100 year ' young' participants of the noble art. However, for competitive bowls, great stamina is required for oft, in blistering heat or freezing weather, players will spend nine to twelve hours a day for five to fourteen days on the green playing two or three games per day.

Zambian bowlers have taken part in many international tournaments (such as the Commonwealth Games) since Independence. In 1986 Zambia were runners-up overall, two points behind Zimbabwe – second in Fours, Triples and Singles – in the Seventh African States Championships in Zimbabwe. Zambia came fourth in the Pairs.

The Zambia Women's Bowling Association came into being at Kapiri Mposhi in 1964 during a meeting between two districts – Copperbelt and the Midlands. At that time the parent body was the Men's Association – the Zambia Bowling Association. The total number of bowlers – Men and Women – was about 800, with eighteen affiliated clubs.

Since 1983, the Zambia Women's Bowling Association has been affiliated in its own right to the National Sports Council of Zambia. There are two districts affiliated to the Zambia Women's Bowling Association:

- The Copperbelt District Women's Bowling Association.
- The Midlands District Women's Bowling Association.

The Copperbelt has eight affiliated clubs, namely Chililabombwe, Nchanga, Chibuluma, Mufulira Mine, Rokana, Roan Antelope, Ndola Bowling and Lawn Tennis Club and Kitwe Playing Fields.

The Midlands have four clubs, namely Broken Hill Mine, Central Sports, Ngwerere and Lusaka Club.

In 1986 about 160 women bowlers were registered in Zambia. National tournaments are played annually.

The Zambia Women's Bowling Association affiliated to the Zambia Olympic, Commonwealth and All-Africa Games Association (ZOCAGA) in 1980.

International Participation

1981 — Women's World Bowls – Canada

1982: Commonwealth Games – Australia. This was the first time women's bowls were played in Commonwealth Games.

Contingent: three, consisting of Sylvia Keeling, Anne Meir and Hilda Hall Playing Triples and were placed fifth overall.

1983 — First African States Tournament – Zambia. Zambia were runners-up

Second African States Tournament – Lobatse, Botswana. Zambia were Singles winner.
Third African States Tournament – Chinhoyi, Zimbabwe.
Fourth African States Tournament – Bulawayo, Zimbabwe. Zambia were Singles winner.

The other nations which participated in this tournament were Swaziland, Zimbabwe, Botswana, Kenya and Malawi.

The later years have seen more and more Zambian women coming into the sport, which is very encouraging, although there is still the difficulty of obtaining Bowls in Zambia.

MOTOR SPORT

Motocross

Motocross was a terminology that only came into use in the seventies, even though popular belief is that it was first coined by the French in 1947. But it is also believed it was the English who first started the sport in 1924 in Surrey and called it 'Scrambling,' the Anglos and all their colonies always referred to it as Scrambling – a motorcycle race held over a cross-country course of about 4.8 kilometres – then, each rider racing flat out to the finish thirty minutes later.

The motorcycle then used was a normal road bike stripped off of its lights instruments et cetera to try and lighten it as much as possible. Most of the engines were English four-strokes, and the motorcycle was a far cry from what they resemble today.

Scrambling was natural pastime in Northern Rhodesia (Zambia) in the forties with most of the roads being dirty and the countryside surrounded with maze or footpaths suitable for Sunday morning exploring.

Imported by the British into Northern Rhodesia in the 1950's a group of jolly gentlemen (most of them policemen or ex Royal Air Force officers) would go for a spiffing scramble on Sunday afternoons. Wearing wooden helmets and R.A.F. goggles, they would cling to their four-stroke bangers along the country paths.

The Eureka Motorcycle Racing Club in Lusaka was founded in the early fifties on the fifty acres of land along the Copper Chalice road where the pioneer Club members built a flat dirty track and later a cross-country dirty track in the centre. Because the old BSA and triumph motorcycles were heavy and with limited suspension, they were more suitable for the outside flat track which was a popular weekend racing activity for many years until the midsixties.

The country saw the emergence of European Bultaco makes and others that were half the weight of the English bikes and had light high horse power two-stroke engines and better suspension that made the bikes fly around the inside cross-country track – called scrambling. Scrambling looked more dangerous, but was in fact safer in terms of slower speeds. But one took a lot of falls before mastering the more difficult technique of staying on one's motorcycle on the rough course that always had a lot of hills, drops and jumps that had to be traversed at high speed to beat opponents.

The sport caught on with amazing popularity among both the commercial farmers, who used their farm bikes, and the town dwellers, who used nearly any kind of motor cycle that they could make suitable. The man that dominated the sport then was the late Bernie Taylor of Ndola, who continued to stay in the sport as a competitor right up to the same year of his death in 1985 at over the age of fifty.

In the early seventies Japanese makes like Honda, Suzuki, Yamaha and Kawasaki found their way into Central Africa, including Zambia.

Events were held in Lusaka, Mazabuka (Tom Reeves' farm), Choma (Joe Brooks' farm), Ndola, Chingola and Mufulira, with the main ones being Lusaka at the Eureka track and Ndola at the Ndola Motor Sports Club.

Young Barry Gough of Kitwe started winning most of these races at that time on a European KTM motorcycle.

The year 1976 saw the first race appearance of young Allan Zaloumis on a red Honda 250 loaned to him by Carlo Comana, who had been king of the flat track racing in Northern Rhodesia and Southern Rhodesia in the fifties riding a BSA Goldstar 500. Zaloumis' debut was something of shock because he came out of nowhere and beat everybody, including Barry Gough. Allan's bike was the latest in terms of motocross (MX) developments, with nearly 15 centimetres of suspension front and rear and a whopping 34 horse power engine.

Zaloumis continued to dominate the sport, but with some years losing the championship to either Brian Pickard or Clive Haagman of Mufulira because of machinery or injury problems.

In 1982 the beautiful clubhouse and track facilities were all lost as the landowner took back the land for resale to another interested partner. But before this happened, Eureka was the venue of a couple of international race events. In 1977 there were three riders from the United Kingdom and in 1980 the Zimbabweans came across as a full team and Allan Zaloumis took the Zambian side to victory on a very exciting July Saturday.

The loss of the Eureka track almost killed the sport as riders had to reluctantly sell their motorcycles to riders on the Copperbelt. Only a handful of persons kept motocross alive in Lusaka, which included Marco Comana, Gary Hindson and Jonathon Nicholson, who would travel to the Copperbelt for race meetings.

In 1985 Solly Patel kindly allowed Marco Comana to build a full size motocross race track on his Chilongolo farm in Makeni. Utilising Patel's Caterpillar bulldozer, Marco carved a two kilometer track on a highside and June 1985 was the first championship date that saw a large crowd of over 3,000 watch some very thrilling racing.

From then on motocross was reborn in Lusaka and rider enthusiasts started acquiring motorcycles. Allan Zaloumis was there at that June 1985 meeting, riding a 1984 Honda 250 and winning all the races. Zaloumis had bought his new motorcycle at cost price from Honda Zambia, but was not in time to capture the 1984 championship, which was held on the Copperbelt, despite winning the remaining race meetings in 1984. That honour had gone to Clive Haagman on a Yamaha 250.

By now the latest bikes were water-cooled horse monsters with 45 horse power and 30.48 centimetres of suspension that allowed them to take 15 metres jumps in top gear with ease.

Ray Wilson was the person most responsible for popularizing the sport in Chingola. He developed a new track on Lufwanyama ranch in 1984 where the next international was held, with Pip Small from England, five Zimbabweans, four Kenyans, one Zairean and thirty local riders taking part at a two-day show. The event was rained on quite heavily, but the show still went on. Pip Small was the fastest, being the 1984 European amateur champion. But the Zambian riders beat them all.

The year 1985 saw Ray Wilson take the crown on his new KTM 250, despite Allan Zaloumis winning most race meetings up to September when he sustained injury while training on his farm.

The year 1986 started with an international competition at Lusaka's Makeni track where five Zimbabweans turned up and two Kenyans. Allan Zaloumis won nearly all the expert races on his ageing 1984 Honda 250, making a fantastic recovery from his injury. Also making a comeback after five years absence was Brian Pickard riding a very outdated bike and just finishing his races.

The first national round was held at the new Chingola track where Allan Zaloumis was absent because of bike problems, but Ray Wilson was closely chased by none other than Barry Gough making a comeback on a 1985 Honda 250. Also making a comeback after not racing since 1984 because of a necessary shoulder operation caused by a racing injury was Marco Comana on a new 1986 Honda 250, which had an amazing 49 horse power. However,

Marco Comana was still trying to find his feet and the rough tiring track proved too much for him as he was overtaken by the Junior champion, Gary Hindson on his new Kawasaki 125 and another fast junior from Chingola, Gary Shiels.

The second round was in Ndola in July and this time motocross saw a very fast Marco Comana shake up Ray Wilson, but Marco was still not fit enough to keep Ray Wilson off his back on the last few laps of each race.

However, the star of the senior experts was not these two, but Brian Pickard on his new Kawasaki 250, sponsored by Nippon Motors, who won all the races and completely upsetting Ray Wilson. Allan Zaloumis, who is now being sponsored by Honda Zambia, could not ride because his new Honda had arrived from Dar-es-Salaam, Tanzania with all its parts missing.

Motor Rallying

Meantime Zambia's motor rallying dates back to the mid-sixties, but with the loss of Shirley Fisher and Ron Gough, it is virtually impossible to be exact. Records do, however, show that the first Zambia National Rally, the nation's greatest motorsports event, was launched in 1969 when Lusaka Motor Sports Club conceived the idea of running an open section rally big enough to attract participants from neighbouring countries. It was planned that the rally should be about 1,600 kilometres long to take place on or around 24 October as part of the independence celebrations. This has been the practice ever since.

By July 1969 it was realized that the rally was not being organized properly. The Club Committee had therefore, to decide whether to cancel the event or to find an alternative organizer. John Ireland of Lusaka Motor sports Club took on the mammoth task of organizing a thirty hour rally covering 1,600 kilometres of exciting terrain. Rallying in Zambia was then in its infancy. Both Lusaka and Ndola Motor Sports Clubs had active rally sections, but those of Nchanga and Roan Antelope were dormant. Kitwe's was virtually non-existent, according to ZMSA records.

The first task besides the obvious one of the planning of the route that John Ireland tacked was that of finding a sponsor. Any rally of that magnitude requires a considerable amount of finance to cover organizational expenses and, more importantly, prizes. Shell and BP Zambia (as it was then known) provided the major part of the sponsorship as they did for the next two years. This, therefore, became known as the Zambia National Shell Rally. The route included such varied section as the near desert conditions near Maala in the Southern Province, where practically fifty kilometers of the route was virtually hidden beneath deep sand, the notorious Zambezi Valley, which has become almost a must, with its sections of twists and turns through steep escarpments and boulder-filled drifts. A few days before the start of the event (which almost caused the cancellation of it) it was discovered that the pontoon at Namwala, a vital river crossing, had broken down and was irrepairable. Thanks to the prompt action of the Government Roads Department, who went out there immediately and filled two outboard motors as a temporary measure, the rally was able to go ahead as planned. Only eight of the eighteen starters crossed the finishing line. The failures were mainly due to the early rains which resulted into wet and hazardous driving conditions.

According to ZMSA records, the rains came with a vengeance and rumours of bogged down vehicles, broken bridges and crunched motors were rife. Among the lucky few finishers were Satwant Singh and John Mitchell, making their debut on the Zambian rally scene. The vehicles used in the rally were of all sorts of makes – from Datsuns to cherished family saloons. The atmosphere was matey rather than competitive, with the half-way stop at Namwala being a social affair as the competitors barbequed meat at 00.04 hours while waiting for the ferry. Datsun won first place and continued to triumph in every rally, with bearded 'Mad Mike' Bond at the wheel and Tim Madrell navigating. Satwant Singh, with John Mitchell navigating came third overall in what was to be the first of string of successful Nationals for them.

Zambia's second national rally in 1970 was organized by Tony Crowder, assisted and abetted by Frank Manning, then Zambia Motor Sports Association president. This event was again organized by Lusaka Motor Sports Club and covered now farmiliar ground in the Central and Southern Provinces including the Zambezi Valley – a favourite section. It also included a special stage on private roads, giving drivers an opportunity to really put their feet down to the floor boards and show their skill. Datsuns once again were victorious, with the team of Bond and Madrell finishing first followed by Seppo Silvennoinen and Brian Moore.

For the third national rally in 1971, organizer Barney Curtis decided to push westwards to Kasempa via the Kafue National Park and along the line of rail to Ndola thus affording the competitors an added bonus of driving through the Park at dawn with spectacular game viewing enroute. Fortunately both cars and animals exercised a health respect for one another and there were no reports of accidents to either cars or animals. The route was dry and high speeds were recorded, with twenty starters completing the race. The rest retired mainly through mechanical failures. The first four cars home were Datsuns with Peter Alexander and Ken Tarplee of Ndola Motor Sports Club taking first and second places and wresting the honours from Lusaka.

The major part of the sponsorship for the fourth national rally in 1972, organized by Ken Lancashire of Ndola Motor Sports Club and Jean Mfuhl was raised by the Lions Club of Itimpi in Kitwe. Due to the increasing prestige and improved publicity, this event attracted several competitors from East Africa, among them were Anne Taieth and Sylvia King who finished in eighth position overall. With the start and finish being changed to Kitwe, with the route passing through Kabwe, Lusaka and most of the Copperbelt towns, a large number of people were able to watch the rally's progress. For the first time the Datsuns were seriously challenged by the Colt Gallants, which took second, fifth and sixth places. The event was won by Satwant Singh and John Mitchell in their Datsun 1600 SSS.

Jim Watson of Lusaka began the initial preparations for the fifth national rally in 1973, but with his imminent departure from Lusaka in September of that year, he handed over the rest of the organization to Bob Rawlinson of Chingola. Rawlinson promptly coerced quite a number of people from clubs into doing something or other, which resulted in a record thirty-eight entries, five of which were from East Africa. The dry road conditions resulting in faster pace meant that many of the crews arrived early at control points. This gave rise to narrower points differences between the first few crews. Guru Singh and Dave Howarth beat Ernie van Leeve and Darrell Hopkins into first place by just one point. Willy Pretorious, who generously loaned the car used to race the route, finished in third place. Pretorious won for himself and navigator Peter Moss, the Zambia Motor Sports Association's Driver and Navigator Championship.

The Colt Gallants once again made a big impression, but could not make the winning slot. Datsuns, as usual, reigned supreme. The 1973 national rally was significant in that it marked the successful finish in any national rally of an indigenous Zambian pair of Rees Ntolongo and Pius Kakungu (later a professional boxing promoter).

For the sixth national rally in 1974, in an endeavour to raise the standard of the rally, Nchanga's Gunther Wendel – an unwilling member of the Club used internationally recognized control boards and printing clocks which helped considerably to alleviate the timing problems experienced in previous rallies. Severe dust problems cut visibility down to virtually zero over most of 2,500 kilometres route, which included the favourite Zambezi Valley and a constructed extension which almost doubled the length of the demanding section. All in all, there were forty-one entries in this rally and it was dominated by the Singh brothers. Satwant eventually came first closely followed by Guru, Peter Alexander came in third and although Annie Taieth and Sylvia King led the field for a considerable length of time, they unfortunately overturned their car quite near the finish and were unable to complete the course.

The organization of the seventh national rally of 1975 by John Ireland presented a different set of problems to that of 1969. With the increase in vehicle power and drive ability coupled with the more professional approach exercised by competitors, this called for a complete re-appraisal of the event's format. This took the form of dispensing with the typical rough car breaking sections and aiming for a faster, more interesting and acceptable competition. The theme adopted for this rally was 'The Fastest Rally in Africa,' which transverse some 2,800 kilometres in under twenty-six hours of driving time.

They then followed an eight-year lull in motor rallying and 1985 the sport was revived in Lusaka. As with the eighth and last rally in 1976, the 1985 competition was organized as an international event which attracted entries from Zimbabwe. Satwant Singh won the event driving an Open Manta.

Some of the notable participants in motor rallying in Zambia, past and present, were, according to Zambia Motor Sports Association's records:

Peter Alexander
1971 Zambia Motor Sports Association champion driver and first Zambian entry ever to finish the East African Safari

John Bousfield
A veteran of the East African, Zambian and even Congolese (Zairean) rallies.

Barney Curtis
Attained a well deserved seventh position in Kenya's Coca-Cola Rally in 1974

Kerry Curtis
Competed in rallies since 1971 with success, being something of a financial whizz-kid. Former Lusaka Motor Sports Club treasurer.

Micky Carle
Won first place in the 1974 Foot Flat in a Datsun or 'Red Bomb,' but unfortunately had engine problems before the start of the Coca-Cola Rally.

Chris Brodie
Navigated for many good drivers and helped Ken Tarple to eighth place in the Coca-Cola Rally. Was second in the Zambia Motor Sports Association competition (Copperbelt) for 1974

Peter Diesveld
A silent character who described his record in 1973 as 'failed.' 1974 proved

better and he came second in the Crest and organized a most enjoyable smooth-running Night Ape Rally. Diesveld maintained his reputation for appearing in unlikely places, the most being the wilds of Northern Kenya during Safari service.

Dave Dickson
A dark horse who rose to fame in Zambia by navigating Barney Curtis to finish fifth place in the 1973 National rally and seventh in the Coca-Cola Rally.

Shirley Fisher
Alias 'Mrs Motor Sport,' was very much involved in rallying from every conceivable angle. In 1974 she was re-elected Zambia Motor sports Association administrative secretary. An unforgettable sight perched on the bonnet of the Colt Gallant driven by teammate, Rasalie van Leeve, in the 1973 National Rally, Shirley and Rosalie were the first Zambian all-woman crew ever to finish a National Rally.

Richard Henman
Progressed from navigating in treasure hunts of the early 1960's to fourth in 1973 Tanzania 1,000 first in the 1973 National Rally, fifth in the Coca-Cola and numerous other placings in company with Guru Singh. Henman organized many club championship rallies for Ndola Motor Sports Club.

John Joanou
Had been a Safari competitor and won high placings in two championship events in 1974.

John Ireland
Connected with motor sport in Zambia for many years and was Director of Motor Sport again in 1974, Navigated for Barney Curtis in the Coca-Cola event.
   I found his articles on rallying most exciting.

Andrew Justice
Navigated for John Joannou.

Ken Lancashire
The 'Big Daddy' of Zambian motor sport, was well known for his articles on press coverage of motoring. Ken Lancashire was described as intrepid traveller.

His descriptionsof some of the more picturesque spots and highways of East Africa (where he competed in many rallies) and writings were also exciting and memorable.

Guilio Luciani

Former Zambia Motor Sports Association champion racing driver. Started rallying in 1972. Whizzed everywhere in his red Lancia in 1974, according to the Zambia Motor Sports Association records.

Alan McKay

An experienced cool, calm and collected navigator. A man of few words. You could be sure that if he said 'Slow down,' he meant it. Was also chairman of Kitwe Motor Sports Club.

Peter Moss

Could not bear to part with his antique VW, in which he started rallying in 1966. Zambia Motor Sports Association champion navigator in 1973. Peter's expertise and luck continued in 1974. He and Bob Rawlinson clicked.

Bob Rawlinson

Had been 'car mad' from birth, then it was rumoured that he emerged holding a spanner! He rallied off and on since 1969 and progressed from an aged Volvo to Colt Gallant. Perhaps his best deserved success was in the 1974 Crest in which he lost brakes, rolled the car then pressed on to win.

Pete Roche

Raced in Zambia for some time and used to regularly clean up all corners on the autocross circuit in his Mini. Started rallying in 1974 and became a driver to be reckoned within a very short time.

Max Scott

Won the class for vehicles between 1300 and 1600 CC in 1973. Was second in Zambia Motor Sports Association competitions in the Midlands.

Guru Singh

Only started rallying in earnest in 1973, when he concluded a successful first season by winning the National Rally. Came fourth in the 1973 Tanzania 1,000, fifth in the 1974 Coca-Cola and drove consistently and well placed in Zambia. Guru Singh also organized training rallies for Lusaka Motor Sports Club of which he was chairman.

Satwant Singh
Has rallied for many years and his record is most impressive. Placings in fourth National rally and a win in 1972. Zambia Motor Sports Association champion driver in 1972, seventh in the East African Safari in 1973, to name but a few of his major achievements. Won the 1985 Zimbabwe Challenge Rally.

Ken Tarplee
A motor sports enthusiast in every sense of the word in preparation in the garage before a rally, competing and supporting the bar afterwards. Came eighth in the Coca-Cola Rally in 1974 and drove well in championship and club rallies. Former Zambia Motor Sports Association treasurer.

Alan Turner
Another convert from racing circles.

Ernie van Leeve
Started rallying with enthusiasm in 1973 and finished his first season by coming second in 1973 National Rally, only missing first position by one point. He had in fact entered the 1974 Safari where he amazed everyone by coming 14th overall (second best private entrant) in the wettest Safari ever. Apart from cleaning some fast sections, van Leeve got by with hardly any slip.

Ken Winter
A hard man to pass. His record in rallying is impressive.

Willie Kasempa and Lance Mutongokwa
Most promising all Zambian team. Kasempa, competition secretary of Lusaka Motor Sports Club, as part of the drive to revive motor sports has organized a number of very successful rallies. Now changing from a Datsun 1200 to well prepared Peugeot 504 Pick-up.

Joe Thompson and Ernest Zebron
Joe and Ernest are a very well matched team. Have been improving gradually and came first in the Lusaka 200 in each rally and they entered. Joe was tired of driving an underpowered Datsun 1200 and changed to a Toyota Celica.

Nick Frangeskides and Mark O'Donnell
New comers to rallying and made a big impact on coming third in the first rally they had entered with the BMW.

Azim Ticklays and S. Patel
Azim is a very fast driver.

Mukesh Patel and Patel
Mukesh surprised everybody on his first attempt by entering the Lusaka 200 very casually with his everyday Peugeot 504 and taking second place.

Vincent Smith and Ian Frieslaar
Very enterprising young pair and have done very well in local rallies with the little Mazda 1300. the pair came first in a training rally and won their class in the Lusaka 200.

Rammy Singh and Dave Thompson
Another upcoming young pair that did extremely well and changed to a Datsun 120Y to a Datsun 160J. Rammy was the only Zambian finisher in the 1986 Zimbabwe Challenge Rally.

Raju Singh
Although a very quick driver, Raju has always been plagued with car trouble since the start of rallying. He has given up the notorious Fiat 131 and shifted to a Datsun 120Y.

O.P. Singh and Wezi Chirwa
Yet another surprise on the rallying scene. Singh entered his little Datsun 1200 in the Sunset/Sunrise Night rally and clinched sixth place overall and won his class on his first attempt.

ZAMBIA NATIONAL RALLY – PAST WINNERS

1969: Clerk of the Course: John Ireland

1st Bond/Madrell	Datsun 1600	
2nd Moore/Silvonnoinen	Datsun 1600	
3rd Singh/Mitchell	Peugeot 404 (East Africa)	
4th Bousfield/Hawke	Volkswagen 1500	
5th Nahon/Omar	Peugeot 404	
5th Stephan/Wiles	Peugeot 204	
7th Preston/Annells	Subaru	
8th Carle/Sharma	Volvo	

1970: Clerk of the Course: Frank Manning

1st Bond/Madrell   Datsun 1600

2nd Singh/Mitchell   Datsun 1600

3rd Seiler/Daun   Datsun 1600

4th Carle/Sharma   Datsun 1600

1971: Clerk of the Course: Barney Curtis

1st Alexander/Price   Datsun 1600

2nd Tarplee/Atkinson   Datsun 1600

3rd Singh/Mitchell   Datsun 1600

4th Bousfield/Bousfield   Datsun 1600

5th Johnston/Dolton   Subaru 1300

1972: Clerk of the Course: Ken Lancashire

1st Singh/Mitchell   Datsun 1600

2nd Winter/Batten   Colt Galant

3rd Alexander/Price   Mazda 616

4th Carle/Stephens   Datsun 1600

5th Pretorius/Moss   Colt Galant

6th Dalseg/Stagg-Macey Colt Galant

1973: Clerk of the Course: Bob Rawlison

1st Guru Singh/Haworth Datsun 1600

2nd Van Leeve/Hoopkins Colt Galant

3rd Pretorious/Moss   Colt Galant

4th Bousfield/McKay   Colt Galant

5th M. Curtis/Dickson   Peugeot 504

6th Carle/Stephens   Datsun 1600

7th Taieth/King   Datsun 1600 (East Africa)

8th Scott/Heaton   Mazda 1300

1974: Clerk of the Course: Gunter Wendel

1st Satwant Singh/Haworth Datsun 710

2nd Guru Singh/Henman   Datsun 1600

3rd Alexander/Burne   Datsun 180B

1975:

1st Satwant Singh/D. Haworth

2nd Carl/Stephens

3rd Rocher/Turne

4th Agas/Calavias

5th Crompton/Gillard
6th Moreli/Waker
7th Giodoti/Parram
8th Joannou/McKay
9th Guru Singh/Mitchell

1976:
1st Guru Singh/Henman
2nd Van-Leeve/Morse
3rd Giodoti/Bennel
4th Olfsen/Oliver
5th Godfrey/Lawson
6th Tarplee/Gibbons
7th Brian/Winter
8th Beaty/Kilby
9th Burns/Camoron
10th Robson/Ciale
11th Burns/Shrimpling
12th Beadwell/Forester
13th Fairweather/Tufuel
14th Walker/Brown

1985:
1st Satwant Singh/Guy Hall   Opel Manta

Figure 23: Lusaka's Muna Singh has won several motor rally titles.

Figure 24: Conquering the motor rally terrain in Zambia.

Figure 25: Time to celebrate... Navigator Fleming Mumba (left) and Muna Singh about to shake hands after winning the 1990 Zambia Motor Sports Association (ZMSA) rally championship.

Figure 26: Zambia's motor rally driver Guru
Singh (right) receiving a trophy.

Figure 27: Muna Singh gearing to take off in a motor rally event.

ATHLETICS

Athletics, the natural sport 'par excellence,' Constitutes the most complete physical training and allows the human-being to satisfy his or her instincts for movement, subject to the discipline of the rules.

Paradoxically, however, the champion – the ultimate example of athletic performance – is a product beyond the norm of human species. Similarly, the world record breaker, even though there may have existed people gifted with greater potential qualities, represents the limit of the human achievement in athletics prowess, measured as it is in space and time.

Scientific researchers, united to practical experience and natural progress, have made athletics to develop to a degree which, in some cases, was never previously dreamt of. However, this process should not justify the means, whose ends are only the achievement of a record to the detriment of the human-being.

Athletics is a physical activity comprising natural actions like walking, running, jumping and throwing. These activities could be categorized as walking races, track and field and cross country. In one way or another, athletics events have been performed by Man since the origin of the species.

Historically, one goes back to classical antiquity where athletics took the form of organized sport. Throughout its development, the athletic programme has been extended and modified, not always in the most rational manner. For example, the distances chosen for the standard races have been derived principally from the English mile, and each speciality has had a different origin.

For this reason, it is a multiple sport which comprises tests that are very different from one another. The various facets of the events differ as much in the method of execution as in the athletic characteristics required for the practice.

Because of its tradition, universality and prestige as well as the wide range of skills and qualities that it encompasses, athletics is the basic sport 'par, excellence.' In addition, it constitutes the most important element of the modern Olympic Games. It is practised in all countries because of its educational value and role in the improvement of the physical condition. It often provides the necessary foundation for optimum performance in other sports. Athletics is often regarded as an example of a country's development.

Apart from the maintenance of a state of physical well-being and personal performance, athletics offers a field of research and experimentation about the human being, with the advantage that progress may be registered in an exact way – time or distance. The scientific fields which are concerned with this sport are therefore wide and varied.

Athletics Events

— *Olympic and World Championship Programme*
The following events (including Heptathlon and Decathlon) and walking are all included in the Olympic and World Championship programmes:

FOR MEN: 100m, 200m, 400m, 800m, 1,500m, 5,000m, 10,000m, 110m hurdles, 400m hurdles, 3,000m steeple chase, 20Km walk, 50Km walk, 4x 100 m relay, 4x400m relay, marathon, high-jumping, long-jump, triple-jump, pole vault, shot-putt, discus, hammer, javelin and decathlon.

FOR WOMEN: 100m, 200m, 400m, 1,500m, 3,00m, 10,000m, 100m hurdles, 400m hurdles, 4x100m relay, 4x400m relay, marathon, 10Km walk high-jump, long-jump, shot-putt, discus, javelin and heptathlon.

— *Running Events*
The official programme comprises eleven individual events and relays of 4x400m arranged in the following groups: sprint and sustained sprint (100m, 200m and 400m), short and middle distance (800 and 1,500m), long distance and steeple chase (5,000m and 3,000m steeple chase), long distance (10,000m and marathon – 42.195 Km), hurdles (110m and 400m).

The short sprint events (100m and 200m) do not encompass a complete circuit of the track. The long sprint (400) is one complete lap. From 800m upwards come the middle and long distance races, all run on the track except the marathon.

— *Field Events*

These comprise two groups of four events: the Jumps (high-jump, long-jump, triple-jump and pole vault) and the throws (shot-putt), discus, javelin and hammer).

At the advent of independence, athletics activities in the then British colony of Northern Rhodesia (Zambia) were governed by the Northern Rhodesia Amateur Athletics and Cycling Association, whose president was G.A. Crane. The Association was founded in 1949 and was the sole governing body for both athletics and cycling activities.

The Association catered mainly for Europeans. The Africans, who were interested in athletics, were under a different orgnisation called the African Athletic Association. This organization was only active on the Copperbelt where it was easy to arrange international tournaments between Africans of Northern Rhodesia and their counterparts from the Katanga region of the then Belgian Congo (Democratic Republic of the Congo). These meetings attracted massive crowds at such places as Scrivener Stadium (Nkana), Kafubu Stadium and Gabbitas Stadium (Nchanga). The main attraction were the sprint 'duels' between Northern Rhodesia's Francis Chilende and the Katangese sprinters. Usually the Northern Rhodesian showed the Katangese sprinters a clean pair of heels.

On 12 April 1964 the Association held an annual general meeting at Ndola's Savoy Hotel. At this crucial meeting, chaired by G.D.A. Crane (the president of the Association), two important decisions were made. The first was that with effect from that date the Association was to discontinue its affiliation to the Rhodesian Amateur Athletics and Cycling Union. The second was the adoption of a new Constitution, which formalized the first decision.

During the April annual general meeting the following officials were elected:

President	G.D.A. Crane
Chairman	B. L. Evans
Vice-Chairman	D. Botha
Secretary	Stan Smith
Treasurer	W.H. Purchase

Committee members - Samson Mubangalala, T.S.A. Haynes

Mubangalala was the first African to be elected as a member of the Executive.

On 5 September 1964, a special general meeting was held at the King George VI High School (now Kabwe Secondary School). During this meeting it was resolved that as from 24 October 1964 the name of the Association would be changed to the Zambia Amateur Athletics Association. This decision meant that the Association would no longer cater for cycling activities.

On 10 January 1965 an Executive meeting was held under the new name. The matters discussed included the Olympic report of the Tokyo Games in which Zambia used two different National Flags – the Union Jack during the opening ceremony and the Zambian Flag at the closing ceremony, Zambia having been born as a sovereign State on 24 October 1964.

The Zambia Amateur Athletics Association's Constitution provides that an Executive Committee comprising the president, chairman, vice-chairman, secretary, assistant secretary, treasurer and area board representatives (2) will be elected at the annual general meeting of the Association for a one year term.

Below are the pioneer officials from 1964 to 1985:

President	G.D.A. Crane
Chairman	B. L. Evans
Vice-Chairman	D. Botha
Secretary	Stan Smith
Treasurer	W.H. Purchase
Committee members	Samson Mubangalala, T.S.A. Haynes
Area board representatives	R. Barnard (Copperbelt), I. Smith (Copperbelt), B Dodd (Midlands).

— *1965:*

President	G.D.A. Crane
Chairman	B. L. Evans
Vice-Chairman	D. Botha
Secretary	Stan Smith
Treasurer	W.H. Purchase
Committee members	T.S.A. Haynes, E. Matale
VicePresidents	Nalumino Mundia, Y.D.E. Dickinson, L. Pavely

G. Crane was elected to life membership of the Association.

— *1966:*

President	G.D.A. Crane
Chairman	B. L. Evans
Vice-Chairman	D. Botha

Secretary	Stan Smith
Treasurer	W.H. Purchase
Committee members	Barnard, W.F. Land, E. Matale

— *1967:*

President	B. L. Evans
Chairman	G. Cuthbertson
Vice-Chairman	Simon Chikwavaire
Secretary/Treasurer	Stan Smith
Assistant/Treasurer	Lt. G.K. Miyanda
Committee members	W.F. Land, E. Matale, M Whittaker

— *1968*

All other positions remained unchanged except the election of E. Matale and A. Spoors as assistant secretary /treasurer and committee member respectively.

— *1969:*

President	G. Urwin
Chairman	Simon Katilungu
Vice-Chairman	Simon Chikwavaire
Secretary/Treasurer	Stan Smith
Assistant Secretary /Treasurer	Captain V. Sifunganyambe
Area board representatives	Yuyi Lishomwa (Midlands), E. Russel (Copperbelt), D. Murphy (Southern Province), A. Nkandu (Copperbelt) Katilungu was the first indigenous person to be elected to the post of chairman.

— *1970:*

President	Arthur Wina

All other positions remained unchanged

— *1971:*

Same as in 1970 except for the election of George Kafula (area board representative – Copperbelt) and B. W. Dodd (area board representative – Midlands).

— *1972:*
Same as in 1971

— *1973:*

President	Arthur Wina
Chairman	Yuyi Lishomwa
Vice-Chairman	Philemon Ngoma
Secretary	Stan Smith
Assistant Secretary	J. Muleya

Area board representatives Miss L. Catchpole (Midlands,) David Ng'andu (Midlands Affiliated National Bodies – Edwin Imboela (Zambia Police)

Liam Sweeney (Zambia Secondary Schools)
Copperbelt Area Board – No representative
National Coach – Samson Mubangalala

In September, the chairman Yuyi Lishomwa, resigned and was replaced by Phillemon Ngoma. Kenneth Chibesakunda was invited to the committee as a vicechairman

In October 1973, Phillemon Ngoma resigned and the Executive Committee resolved that Kenneth Chibesakunda act as chairman until the next meeting of the Executive could be held, attended by the president and to which Ngoma would be invited.

The assistant secretary/treasurer also resigned.

— *1974:*

President	Arthur Wina
Chairman	Philemon Ngoma

Except for the vacant position of assistant secretary/treasurer, all other positions remained unchanged.

— *1975:*

President	Arthur Wina
Chairman	Philemon Ngoma
Vice-Chairman	Kenneth Chibesakunda
Secretary/Treasurer	Stan Smith
Assistant Secretary /Treasurer	Johannes Mparuri
Copperbelt	No representative

National Coach	Samson Mubangalala

In October 1975, Stan Smith suspended himself from office and his action was endorsed by the Executive Committee which met to discuss his case. After a lengthy search for a replacement, Bannie Lombe was coopted as acting secretary/treasurer. His cooption was endorsed at the 1976 annual general meeting held at the President's Citizenship College in Kabwe.

— *1976:*

The Association's Constitution was amended to provide for the splitting of the functions of the secretary and treasurer. Accordingly, the election of officers put the following into effect:

President	Arthur Wina
Chairman	Philemon Ngoma
Vice-Chairman	Kenneth Chibesakunda
Secretary	Bannie Lombe
Vice Secretary	Samson Mubangalala
Treasurer	Stephen Mwamba
Copperbelt	W. Mulenga, George Kafula
Midlands	Nicodemus Maipambe, Johannes Mparuri
National Association	David Ng'andu (Zambia Higher Institutions Sports Association (ZHISA)

— *1977:*

As in 1976, the only change being the resignation of Samson Mubangalala as Vice-Secretary in order to concentrate on coaching.

— *1978:*

President	Arthur Wina
Chairman	Kenneth Chibesakunda
Vice-Chairman	Johannes Mparuri
Secretary	Bannie Lombe
Vice Secretary	Ziezi Limbambala
Treasurer	George Kafula
Copperbelt	P. Banda, W. Mulenga
Midlands	Nicodemus Maipambe, Godfrey Mwanza
National Bodies	David Ng'andu (ZHISA)
National Coach	Samson Mubangalala

At one of the Executive meetings held during the early part of 1978, it was resolved that Sikota Wina be invited to accept the post of Chairman of the Association. The offer was accepted and Sikota Wina chaired one Executive meeting later in the year and resigned the following year. Sikota Wina thus goes on record as the Zambia Amateur Athletics Association Chairman who served the shortest period in office. Kenneth Chibesakunda assumed the duties of acting chairman. Mwamba resigned as treasurer and George Kafula was subsequently elected treasurer.

— *1979:*

President	Arthur Wina
Chairman	Kenneth Chibesakunda
Vice-Chairman	Johannes Mparuri (acting)
Secretary	Bannie Lombe
Vice Secretary	Ziezi Limbambala
Copperbelt	P. Banda, W. Mulenga
Midlands	G. Banda
National Coach	Samson Mubangalala

In August 1979 Samson Mubangalala resigned and was later replaced by Misheck Mwale.

— *1980:*

As in 1979, the constitution was amended to provide for the term of office for Executive Committee members to be extended to four years.

— *1981:*

President	Arthur Wina
Chairman	Stan Smith
Vice-Chairman	Leonard Shamoya
Secretary	Samson Mubangalala
Vice Secretary	Ziezi Limbambala
Treasurer	George Kafula
Copperbelt	P. Banda, P. Mpondwa
Midlands	Godfrey Mwanza
National Bodies	Major B. L. Lungu
National Coach	Mischeck Mwale
Athletes' Representatives	Nicodemus Maipambe, Sylvia Chesterman, Coreen Hatembo.

Samsom Mubangalala, Dave Lishebo and Charles Lupiya elected as life members.

— *1985:*

President	
Chairman	Arthur Wina
Vice-Chairman	John Mufalali
Secretary	Mischeck Mwale
Vice Secretary	Godfrey Mwanza
Treasurer	George Kafula
Vice-Treasurer	vacant
Copperbelt	vacant
Midlands	vacant
Athletes' representatives	vacant

Stan Smith elected life member.

The Zambia Amateur Athletics Association was admitted to the East African Athletics Board in 1969. This action was a result of the application for membership which was submitted in 1968 by Stan Smith in his capacity as ZAAA secretary. The application was submitted during the Marathon Championships held in Tanzania to which Zambia was invited.

Before its membership of the Board, Zambia's exposure to international competition had been restricted to an annual athletics competition with Southern Rhodesia (Zimbabwe). This competition (the Clark Cup) was held on a rotational basis, with venues alternating between Salisbury (Harare) and Lusaka.

In November 1965 Southern Rhodesia declared Unilateral Declaration of Independence (UDI). This development meant that Zambia had now been cut off from the only international tournament that the nation was using to groom its young athletes. The Clark Cup competition, therefore, came to an end in 1965 with the last competition having been held at Matero Stadium in Lusaka in July 1965 and which was won by Southern Rhodesia.

The East African Athletics Board was formed in 1934, initially between Kenya and Uganda. Tanzania joined the Board in 1955. In 1968 the application for Zambia Amateur Athletics Association to join the Board was accepted and accordingly Zambia was invited to the championships scheduled for August 1969 in Uganda.

In July 1969 Zambia athletes converged at Matero Stadium in Lusaka to compete for places in the national team to travel to Kampala for the 1969 version of the East African Athletics Championships. The trials at Matero attracted a large entry and all events were keenly contested, bringing together 249 athletes from all corners of the Republic.

After a considerable amount of jostling, the Zambian national team of thirty-four men and twenty-five women was finally selected. The team was to be led by the secretary, Stan Smith as Team Manager. Catherine Namfukwe (now Mrs Catherine Pamba), with Samsom Mubangalala and Jane Chikambwe as Chaperon, male and female captains respectively. The team coach was James Walubita from the Ministry of Education.

At the close of the trials at Matero Stadium the ZAAA was short of K1,500 of the required sum to charter an aircraft from Zambia Airways. After Smith's appeal the shortfall was quickly raised.

The BAC 1-11 took off on a beautiful Wednesday morning amid the gasps of astonishment from the youthful Zambian athletics team comprising mainly of students and twelve working class athletes. The flight was a wonderful experience for some and a nightmare for others. The smooth touch-down at Entebbe Airport after a two-hour flight was a very welcome feature. The two days before the championships were spent on getting acclimatized. The championships began with pomp and splendour on Friday afternoon, with a full programme of events. By the time the championships ended on Sunday, the Zambian team had been reduced to a despondent and thoroughly outclassed lot – having achieved only four medals – three silver and one bronze.

In winning these three silver medals through Jane Chikambwe (100m and 200m) and Christine Kabunda (80m hurdles), the women's team was placed third, managing only to beat an equally unimpressive Tanzanian team, the Kenyans being the overall winners.

The Zambian men's team managed only a bronze medal through Jessyman Wishkoti (10.6 secs in 100m) and were placed last in the competition. To many athletes in the Zambian team these championships were a very disturbing notice of the impeding struggle along the ranks of the have-nots of African track and field when apparently the nation has tremendous national talent in the running events. The writing on the wall in Kampala was clear. Zambia was lagging behind in athletics and unless something tangible was undertaken, the performance gap between the East Africans and the Zambians would continue to widen. One of the most interesting aspects of the East African teams was their composition, mainly with mature athletes from the defence forces, the police and prison services. These athletes had been exposed to international tours of Europe and the Oceania. Some of them had even managed to win medals in the Olympic Games in 1968 in Mexico (Kipchoge Keino 1,500m Gold medal), 5,000m (Silver), Amos Biwot, 3,000m (Gold), Naftati Temu, 10,000m (Silver) and 4x400m (Silver medal).

The outstanding performer in the Zambian team was undoubtedly a shy looking but determined student from St. Joseph's Secondary School in Monze, Jane Chikambwe. Chikambwe, who was the female captain demonstrated such aggression in running as never before in East Africa, succumbing only to Uganda's Judith Ayaa, who had to break the East African sprint records in order to overcome the Zambian. Chikambwe's performance earned her the honour of being interviewed on both radio and television in the evening. On return to Lusaka, many questions pre-occupied the Zambian team members – to quit or not to quit, with quitting being the best alternative as 'not quitting' entailed hard work and self-sacrifice which was beyond an average Zambian athlete.

The subsequent participation by the Zambian athletes in these championships, which later became known as the East and Central African Athletics Championships made little impact and the performance of the athletes in the domestic meetings showed insignificant improvement. The rest of the performance results by Zambians in the above championships are as follows:

— *1970:*

    Contingent: forty-five athletes   Coaches: E. Chintu, S. Jere.
    Gold   -   Nil
    Silver   -   Nil
    Bronze   -   Loveness Kamanga (Long-jump)

— *1971: Lusaka, Zambia*

    Contingent: Sixty-five athletes   Coaches: Samson Mubangalala

    F. M. Simwinga and E. Chintu
    Gold   -   Audrey Chikani (Mrs Muhundika)
    Silver   -   Jane Chikambwe (200m)
    Inonge Nganga (Shot-putt)
    Audrey Chikani (High-jump)
    Women's relay (4x400m)
    Bronze – Jacques Kalisirira (High-jump)
    Beatrice Lungu (Mrs Cains)
    Christeta Chibamba (Javelin)

— *1972: Dar-es-Salaam, Tanzania*

    Contingent: thirty-three athletes   Coaches: Simon Chikwavaire
    Gold   -   John Kambole (Marathon)
    Grace Munene   -   (200m)
    Silver   -   Audrey Chikani (Long-jump)

Jessie Chikoko   -   (Pentathlon)
Bronze   -   Women's relay (4x100m)

— *1975: Mombasa, Kenya*
Contingent: twenty-four athletes
Gold   -   Bogger Mushanga (Long-jump)
Silver   -   Nil
Bronze   -   David Lishebo (110m hurdles)

— *1976: Zanzibar, Tanzania*
Contingent: thirty-six athletes   Coach: Samson Mubangalala
Gold   -   Carol Mumbi (High-jump)
Silver   -   Bogger Mushanga (Long-jump)
Carol Mumbi   -   (Mrs Sikwawi) (Long-jump)
Bronze   -   Men's relay (4x400m)
Women's relay (4x100m)

— *1979: Mombasa, Kenya*
Contingent: thirty-five athletes   Coach: Samson Mubangalala
Gold   -   Bogger Mushanga (Triple-jump)
Silver   -   David Lishebo (110m hurdles)
Carol Mumbi   -   (High-jump)
Bronze   -   Bogger Mushanga (Long-jump)
David Lishebo   -   (400m hurdles)

Following the request by the Zambia Olympic, Commonwealth and All-Africa Games Association, the Zambia Amateur Athletics Association Executive met in September to select athletes for the Second All-Africa Games to be held in Lagos, Nigeria, starting on 8 January 1973. In an unprecedented action the ZAAA used a criterion of selection, rating nine women athletes in the order of merit listing. Consequently, the final team of eight athletes comprised only women athletes, namely:

Beatrice Lungu (100m and 400m)
Grace Munene (200m and 400m)
Beauty Banda (800m)
Mary Mulenga (800m and 1,500m)
Mary Ng'andwe (1,500m)
Audrey Chikani (Long-jump and High-jump)
Jessie Chikoko (High-jump)

Shirley Mweemba (Javelin)
Samson Mubangalala (Coach)

The Second All-Africa Games in Lagos were the first for the Zambian athletes, having been left out of the two-man boxing team to the first All-Africa Games in 1965 in Congo-Brazzaville. Although the team lacked experience required for a competition of this magnitude, the girls responded well to the tough competition, with four athletes – Mary Mulenga, Mary Ng'andwe, Audrey Chikani and Beauty Banda – making it to the finals of their respective events. Mubangalala reached the finals also.

The girls broke the national records in their events as follows:

Beauty Banda	800m	(2m 19.5 secs)	(2m 21 secs)	8
Mary Mulenga	800m	(2m 16.2 secs)	(2m 21 secs)	6
Mary Mulenga	1,500m	(4m 48.5 secs)	(5m 1 sec)	5
Mary Ng'andwe	1,500m	(4m 52 secs)	(5m 1 sec)	6
Audrey Chikani	Long-jump	(5.57m)	(5.55m)	4

In addition to results two Zambian sprinters – Beatrice Lungu and Grace Munene – reached the semi-finals in 100m and 200m respectively. This improvement in the performance of athletes was attributed to the ten day camp in Kabwe.

The results in the competition pleased many people in the ZAAA Committee and underlined the need for residential training before major games. The fourth placing of Audrey Chikani was particularly impressive. The Third All-Africa Games were held in July 1978 in Algiers, Algeria. The country's economic situation having deteriorated badly necessitated the reduction in the number of athletes in preference to more boxers. A team of four athletes was inducted into the All-Africa Games Zambian team. These were:

Bogger Mushanga (Long and Triple-jump)
Ngwira Musonda (Marathon and 10,000m)
Patrick Chiwala (10,000m)
Violet Mulobeka (Mrs Kangwa) (800m)

Coach: Samson Mubangalala

The performance at the All-Africa Games by athletes from all the countries represented showed a marked improvement. This resulted into national records of various countries falling like leaves in Autumn.

Generally, the Zambian athletes acquitted themselves impressively, with Musonda grabbing a fifth placing in the marathon, beating the eventual Commonwealth Games Gold medalist, Gidemius Shibanga of Tanzania. In the Triple-jump and the Long-jump, Bogger Mushanga, was unlucky not to have at least managed a bronze. His fifth placing both in the Triple and Long-jump clearly demonstrated the potential that he was endowed with. In being placed fifth, he had to break the national records in the two events with 15.54m (Triple-jump) and 7.54m (Long-jump). Mushanga who, to date is the best long/triple-jumper had to struggle with the additional responsibility of being the Police Coach and National Coach.

Mulobeka, the lone female athlete, performed well. She managed to achieve a new national record of 2m 15.2 secs (electrically), making it to the semi-finals of her event. The statistical data on the performance of the Zambian athletes in the All-Africa Games is as follows:

— *1973:*

    Contigent: eight athletes   Coach: Samson Mubangalala

Gold	-	Nil
Silver	-	Nil
Bronze	-	Nil

    Placings of Zambian athletes:

    Audrey Chikani – fourth in Long-jump final

    Beauty Banda – eighth in 800m final

    Mary Mulenga – sixth in 800m final and fifth in1,500m final

    Mary Ng'andwe - sixth in 1,500m

    Beatrice Lungu - eliminated in semi-final

    Jessie Chikoko – failed to qualify for final

    Grace Munene – eliminated in the semi-final

    Shirley Mweemba failed to qualify for final

— *1978: Algiers, Algeria*

    Contigent: four athletes

Gold	-	Nil
Silver	-	Nil
Bronze	-	Nil

    Placings of Zambian athletes:

Bogger Mushanga	-	fifth in triple and long-jump final
Ngwira Musonda	-	fifth in marathon
Violet Mulobeka	-	eliminated in semi-final
Patrick Chiwala	-	not placed in 10,000m (miscalculated laps)

COMMONWEALTH GAMES

Zambia athletes during that period had taken part in four meetings of the Commonwealth Games, starting with the 1970 Games at Edinburgh, Scotland, through to the Brisbane Games in 1982. In between, the Zambian athletes have featured in the 1974 Games in Auckland, New Zealand, and the 1978 Games at Edmonton, Canada. Zambia withdrew from 1986 Edinburgh Games held in Scotland.

Generally the performance by the Zambian athletes in the Commonwealth Games left much to be desired except for athletes such as David Lishebo, Jessyman Wishkoti and Bogger Mushanga. The performance of the above named athletes will be featured separately.

— *1970: Edinburgh, Scotland*
Contingent – eleven athletes Coach: F. Simwinga

The surprise of these games was the brilliant performance of Jessyman Wishkoti who became the first Zambian athlete to make it to the semi finals of a track event, reaching the 100m semi-finals with a new national record of 10.5secs (electrically). Of late, Dave Lishebo has been credited with this distinction erroneously. Lishebo became the second athlete to reach a semi-final of a track event in the 1982 Commonwealth Games.

Gold	-	Nil
Silver	-	Nil
Bronze	-	Nil

The rest of the athletes were eliminated in the preliminary rounds.

— *1974 — Auckland, New Zealand*
Contingent – eleven athletes Coach: Nu

Charles Lupiya and Rogers Chella were entered in the 100m, with Charles Lupiya being entered in the long-jump as well. Eliminated in the qualifying round.

Gold	-	Nil
Silver	-	Nil
Bronze	-	Nil

— 1978: Edmonton, Canada

Contingent – four athletes   Coach: Samson Mubangalala

Violet Mulobeka (400m), Bogger Mushanga (long-jump and triple-jump), Ngwira Musonda (marathon) and Patrick Chiwala (marathon).

Mulobeka was eliminated in the preliminaries. Mushanga was eliminated in the qualifying round of the triple-jump. He however qualified to the finals in the long-jump and set a national record of 7.69, which is unbroken to date. Mushanga was placed seventh in the finals and this is the highest placing of any Zambian in the Commonwealth games. He is the only one so far who has reached the final of his event in these Games.

In the past, people have always talked of David Lishebo as being the highest placed in the Commonwealth Games when, in fact, it is Mushanga. Musonda and Chiwala performed badly and were placed below thirty-fifth position.

In terms of the medal tally:

Gold	-	Nil
Silver	-	Nil
Bronze	-	Nil

1982: Brisbane, Australia

Contingent – nine athletes   Coach: Misheck Mwale

These games brought back refreshing memories of the Edinburgh Games twelve years earlier. The games not only saw another Zambian athlete working himself to the semi-finals of his event, but in doing so David Lishebo became the first Zambian athlete to win his heat in any track event. Lishebo won his heat with an impressive 47.45 seconds in the 400m. The only female athlete in the team, Hilda Musopa, was eliminated in her first round heat. Her time of 2 minutes 10.5 seconds was a new national record.

The placings of Zambian athletes were as follows:

David Lishebo – semi-finals 400m
Dick Kunda – eliminated in second round heat
Charles Lupiya – eliminated in second round heat

Henry Ngolwe – eliminated in second round heat
John Banda - eliminated in second round heat
Charles Kachenjela - eliminated in second round heat
Archfellow Musango - eliminated in second round heat
Hilda Musopa - eliminated in second round heat

The Zambian 4 x 400m relay team comprising David Lishebo, Charles Lupiya, Lyamba Nyambe and Dick Kunda featured in the finals due to less teams entering this event. The quartet were placed sixth in the final.

Gold	-	Nil
Silver	-	Nil
Bronze	-	Nil

Although Zambia has now earned herself the tag of 'Olympic Veteran,' having participated in the 1964, 1968, 1972, 1980, 1984 and withdrawing from the 1976 Montreal Olympics, the performance of its athletes at the Olympic Games can best be described as disappointing. In the Games, the Zambian athletes have continued to put up performances which gives one the impression that mediocrity is their predicament. This trend was set in 1964 at the Tokyo Olympics.

Most, if not all, Zambian top athletes have been trained by expatriate coaches and these are as follows:

Benson Mulomba, Ambrose Miyanda and Raymond Lweendo – Neil Champion.
Beatrice Lungu – Nigel Cains (whom she later married)
Grace Munene, Jane Chikambwe, Beatrice Lunda, Charity Himabulo – John McLauglin
Audrey Chikani, Jessie Chikoko – Peter Dann
Carol Mumbi – Sylvia Chesterman
Jessyman Wishkoti – Expatriate Army Coach

The exceptions to these successes by expatriate coaches were the grooming of David Lishebo, Charles Lupiya, Batwell Tembi, Amon Nyaundi, Janet Lubwika, Beauty Banda, Thelma Finchman, Dick Kunda, Violet Mulobeka and Imasiku Sitali into national Champions by Samson Mubangalala.

Zambia participated in five meetings of the Olympic Games with one withdrawal in 1976. These were as follows:

— *1964: Tokyo, Japan*
Contingent – five athletes

Wally Bob (110m hurdles) – last in his heat, Jeff Smith (100m and 200m) – last in his heats, Laurent Chifita (marathon) – did not finish, Zoom Kapambwe (marathon) forty-first position and Trevor Haynes (marathon) – did not finish).
Results:

Gold	-	Nil
Silver	-	Nil
Bronze	-	Nil

— *1968: Mexico City, Mexico*
Contingent – three

Enock Mweemba (marathon) – fortieth position, John Kalimbwe (marathon) – forty-fifth position and Douglas Sinkala (marathon) – thirty-fifth position.

These games are remembered more for the death of the delegation leader, Graham Cuthbertson, in Mexico City than for the performance of the athletes.
Results:

Gold	-	Nil
Silver	-	Nil
Bronze	-	Nil

— *1972: Munich, West Germany*
Contingent – seven

Beatrice Lungu (200m) – sixth position of seven, Grace Munene (400m) – last out of eight, Audrey Chikani (long-jump) – eliminated in qualifying round, Benson Mulomba (1,500m) – sixth position, Nicodemus Maipambe (400m) – last position, Ngwira Musonda (5,000m) – last position and was almost lapped by the leading runners. Lameck Mukonde (100m) – pulled a muscle and did not complete.
Results:

Gold	-	Nil
Silver	-	Nil

Bronze - Nil
— *1976: Montreal, Canada*
Zambia joined the Afro-Arab withdrawal in protest against the participation of New Zealand.

— *1980: Moscow, Soviet Union*
 Contingent – eight
  Charles Kachenjela (100m) – eliminated, Charles Lupiya (400m) – advanced to quarter finals. Sidney Muziyo (200m) (200m) – eliminated in first round, Bogger Mushanga (triple-jump) – eliminated in qualifying round, Archfellow Musango (800m) – eliminated, David Lishebo (400m hurdles) eliminated, Ngwira Musonda (10,000m) – eliminated and Gabriel Halwando (marathon) – thirty-fifth position.

These games also witnessed the boycott by the United States of America and her allies.
 Results:

Gold - Nil
Silver - Nil
Bronze - Nil

— *1984: Los Angeles, United States of America*
 Contingent – four
  Mutale Mulenga (High-jump) – eliminated in qualifying round, Henry Ngolwe (100m and 200m) – eliminated, Archfellow Musango (800m and 1,500m) – eliminated, David Lishebo (400m) – reached the semi-finals.

The games in Los Angeles revealed one important aspect of the need to subject Zambian athletes to systematic and long-term training programmes if they were to perform well at future Olympic games. Lishebo's performance demonstrated this fact. He had trained under one coach for more than twelve years and his training was carefully evaluated at regular intervals and where necessary revised. Lishebo goes on record as the only Zambian athlete to reach a semi-final in the Olympic games. He has also earned himself the distinction of being the only Zambian athlete at both the Commonwealth and Olympic Games to come first in his heat.

Ironically, both Lishebo and Charles Lupiya (the 1980 Olympics quarter-finalists) were coached by Samson Mubangalala from 1971 onwards.

And to sum up various performances by Zambian athletes, Godfrey Mwanza, Zambia Amateur Athletics Association vice-secretary said, 'the Executive looked at Zambia's poor performances during the past international fora like the Commonwealth and Olympic Games and regional competitions like the East African Championships. One of the factors which led to this dilemma was the non-availability of incentives and this resulted in apathy on the part of sportsmen and women. Eventually, those that took up serious competition at club level became frustrated and hung up their spikes, thus lowering the morale of upcoming athletes.

This chapter on athletics would be incomplete without mentioning Zambia's departed hero, Yotham Muleya, who died in the United States of America in 1959. Yotham Muleya was the fourth surviving son of Jamu Siakwambwa and his wife Munsanda. Because his immediate elder brother died in infancy. Yotham was named Siachobe. According to Tonga custom, the surviving child from a number of elder brothers or sisters who die in infancy is given a name of anything except human. In the case of Yotham, his name was derived from a beetle, but this was a beetle with a difference. This was the herald, the harbinger of good news.

Yotham's grandfather, Mudukula, was a rain-maker – a really famous one, and not a charlatan at that. The family was, therefore, well versed in the rain cult. Thus, the name Siachobe was taken from a beetle which is associated with rain. For the outset of the rainy season and with the first rains, all sorts of insects celebrate the first drops of water and come out of hiding. In time of drought or late rains, each time children saw beetle Siachobe, they could form a circle around him and ask 'Coombe imvwula ili kuli?' meaning 'beetle where is the rain?' It is an insect that nobody kills but rather revers. It is John the Baptist, to Jesus as what Siachobe is to rain. It heralds hope. Siachobe's birth gave his parents resigned hope and anxiety. Hope that he would live and anxiety in case, like the others, he did not live.

Yotham, who I shall refer to as Siachobe, started his education at Mudukula Primary School at Mudukula Village, Chief Moyo in Choma district. He received much encouragement from his eldest brother, Jonathan, an educationist himself. Jonathan Muleya at the time had already set his career to that of being a teacher. He was at Chalimbana doing his teacher training. Siachobe's other elder brother, White Muleya, had already started teaching as a lower primary school teacher and lay preacher. The two played a leadership role for Yotham to emulate.

In this regard the two brothers had set two sets of standards. Jonathan

Muleya reached matriculation being the eldest brother, his academic qualifications were a standard yardstick for his younger brothers and sisters to emulate. Jonathan Muleya was and has been the brainest member of the family, blessed with photographic memory. He also made it clear that he expected no less achievements from his younger brothers. If you were not good at school, he certainly would not accept any kind of explanation and his brothers were all grateful for his uncompromising position towards education.

From White Muleya, Yotham Muleya received the challenge of physical strength, agility and practical achievement. White was renowned to be bull tamer. He would single-handedly wrestle with a bull until he subdued it. From an early age, Yotham Muleya chased calves into submission, tied them up only to release them again. While heading cattle, he excelled in various competitions such as spear throwing and kamando (a form of body wrestling). Athletics came to him rather naturally.

His father complemented by his mother were a fort of discipline and love. Yotham Muleya was as loved as he was adored. The anxiety created by the early deaths of his elder brothers and sisters seemed to have created a special place for Siachobe in his family. Even with Jamu Siakwamba's unfailing discipline, Yotham was his soft spot. Against the background of loving supportive parents, an athletic and a genious of a brother, the setting was made for Yotham Muleya to go into the world, beyond the immediate confines of his family, with self confidence and zeal.

Yotham Muleya's athletic career started at Sikalongo Mission in Choma. From the time he was in Standard Three, he was no match for his agemates. Those days there was little distinction between the younger and the older boys. You all competed together for the same events. Sichobe was too small for the short distances. He could not effectively compete with the older boys. In the longer distances, however, his stamina could hold out and beat the older boys into submission. He, therefore, settled down to specialize in the two kilometers races. His immediate rival was his cousin Moses Muleya. He too was tall, lanky and had the speed of a whirlwind. With these qualities, Yotham Muleya left Sikalongo Mission an accomplished athlete at the age of fifteen and entered competitive sport at Munali Secondary School in Lusaka.

Yotham Muleya had a younger brother, Jesse Muleya, the youngest in the family. 'I was the only one he pitted against when he was home on school vacation. I remember how we used to run together when he wanted to teach me to be a good athlete.' Jesse Muleya said. 'He would let me go ahead of him say about 200 metres and then shout start! He would stay behind with the dogs and race with them towards me, while I was attempting with all my energy to run away from him. Siachobe could run so fast that he would catch up with me before I could do another 200 metres. After overtaking me the dogs racing him would already show strain. At the end of the race, the dogs would be coughing from the dust raised while Siachobe would be laughing at both me and the dogs for being inept. He would mock me and I did not like it. It made me try harder and harder believing I would eventually beat him. I never had the chance.'

When he needed to seriously train for endurance, Yotham would leave early in the morning for a 16 kilometres cross-country run. Mudukula Village is on a hilly area and ideal for training and uphill running. In spite of all this running around it was not obvious to the neighbouring villagers that Yotham was practising every morning. He did not exhibit his training. It was a private affair. In traditional village life there was no aimless sport. All sport was practical and purposeful. Young boys were involved in spear throwing competitions for both distance and accuracy, in wrestling for body building and stamina and in boxing. All sport was to prepare the child for self-defence or for preparation into adulthood. Apart from Jesse Muleya who shared his practices, nobody else in the village ever saw Yotham Muleya run as fast as he did. All they saw were pictures in the Intanda newspaper, published in Tonga.

The Intanda assumed even greater significance in 1958 when there were pictures everywhere of Yotham Siachobe Muleya wearing a black short and a white vest. He was shown running ahead of a whiteman. He was not running away. He had beaten Gordon Pirie to a race, just like he had beaten the dogs.

It was not new to Jesse but normal. Jesse was on his school holiday when photographers arrived at Mudukula Village. They were accompanied by reporters. They hastily looked for Yotham's younger brother, and Jesse came forward. They asked Jesse to gather his playmates, which he did in no time. Jesse was very excited to be given these chores. Jesse enjoyed performing useful functions, achieving targets and being sent was one of those roles which gave one the opportunity to prove his ability to perform and make greater achievements.

While Jesse was gathering his playmates, somebody was talking to his parents while another was taking pictures. It was all fascinating to Jesse. When attention was again drawn to Jesse, he was asked to stand abreast with his playmates and to run towards a photographer when he gave the signal. At the fall of his arm they raced towards him and without design, completely unintended, Jesse beat his playmates to his race. The camera registered this result and the next thing that happened was that Jesse saw his picture in the Intanda ahead of his playmates with the headings: 'The younger brother beats all the children in the village.' 'We were all covered by the newspaper men. If they told my parents they did not reveal that this was for a newspaper. If we knew we would have worn our Sunday best clothes and probably we could have run faster,' Jesse said.

A week later Yotham Muleya arrived home from Lusaka and his race in Salisbury (Harare). It was Christmas time. On Christmas Eve there was drumming, dancing and excitement of all kinds. There were snacks and refreshments for the festive season. Yotham decided to show his village folk what a good successful athlete could do. He gave the audience a sample of exercises. He began with press-ups and belly bending. He only took about five minutes after the end of the exercise, he counted in the starter's position and mock sprinted ten paces only and stopped explaining that, that was how he prepared for the races. The villagers who had been spell-bound were now filled with awe and the fun was over. They felt that their Siachobe tortured himself beyond need. The whiteman must be making him do all this. One by one they walked away from the Christmas party.

The party ended prematurely. Yotham Muleya regretted his demonstrations, but it was too late. They went to sleep and the left over food was given to whoever needed it.

The following day on Christmas day those who had been at the party spread rumours that Yotham could run so fast he would catch a duiker. They told stories of how he glows in the dark when he is preparing to run, and how no human-being could outrun him. He became conversational and topical.

Then the hero went abroad and what followed was bad news. Yotham Muleya had died in a car accident, far away in the whiteman's land. The same Yotham who had out-sprinted another whiteman exactly a year before. He must have been killed by the whiteman. The whole village, the neighbouring villages, gathered at his parents' home before his body arrived. They wailed and mourned helplessly for their departed hero. It was incredible as it was incredulous. He did not make it to the 1959 Christmas. He was only heading on his final trip home from where he had come. He had made a mock sprint of the ten paces, he lived another ten months and he was dead. The coffin carrying his body finally arrived, stopping at Sikalongo Mission for the church service commending him into the hands of God for he was a God-fearing man. After the service, and at a piece of ground selected by Jamu Siakwambwa, his father, a hole was dug for his grave, his final resting place. When the pall-bearers arrived with the coffin bearing his body, the villagers went into fits of frenzy. Only a Christmas before, they had a wonderful party with Yotham, the handsome athlete, their hero, their son, their brother, cousin, friend and all, now he was reduced to the air-tight box, his coffin. It could not be real, yet it was. The din of mourning was overwhelming and deafening for a true hero.

The Government played its part in burying the country's hero. He was given a State funeral and Jesse Muleya represented the family at the open air memorial service which was held at Hodgson Technical College, now David Kaunda Technical College. It was a farewell given to a hero who eroded the invincibility of the whiteman publicly for all to see.

Figure 28: Zambian international athlete Samuel
Matete captured in the men's 400m hurdles.

Figure 29: Samuel Matete carrying the Zambian flag after winning the world's 400m hurdles. He was the second fastest man in the world over this distance.

WRESTLING

Wrestling in all fairness, was made popular in Zambia (Northern Rhodesia) by the late Fred Coates. It was, at that time, a predominantly whiteman's game, save for John Chipeta on the Copperbelt and Tennison Phiri in the Midlands. It died down after a while but picked up again when Nigerian 'Power Mike' (real name Mike Okpara) decided to arouse Coates from 'retirement' and challenged him to a showdown.

Wrestling, a game of grapplers on a mat, perhaps reached its highest peak in Zambia in the early 1970's. Instrumental in this were promoters like Nic Nichol, Daniel Katungu, Philip Nhekairo, Bronco Promotions, Gibson Nwosu and Paul Fisher, to name but a few. At about the same time Donald Lightfoot and his colleagues also joined the promoter's ranks when they brought into the country a team of huge wrestlers. Among these wrestlers were people like Prince Kumali and Rudi Satuski. The tour was a grest success, so much that a good number ofo Zambians were attracted to the sport. From the Copperbelt came, inter alia, John Chipeta and Hugo Mulenga. From the Midlands, together with Jackie Karamel, came Willie 'Tiger Boy' Nkandu, acrobatic Larry Old, Andrew Mubanga, Harjot Singh, John Chipeta and Philip Thompson as coach.

The Zambian public were treated to first class entertainment bhy local and foreign wrestlers. They included Coates, Power Mike, Barry Lindo, Hungarian Josef Kovacs, British Mid-heavyweight Colyn Jonson, Veejay Kumar, Dalbir Singh, Chief Whitecloud (son of chief Bold Eagle) ruler of the Arizona Rocky Mountain Pass, Danny Lynch, Terry Rudge, Masambula and Clive 'Iron Fist' Myers.

Like his father, Chief Billy Whitecloud hated all whitemen. The other international wresters who fought in Zambia were 'The Destroyer' from America (the most hated wrestler) and public enemy number one. Tony St

Clair, the handsome and scientific wrestler from the United Kingdom Johnny Saint, Butcher Mason (the 'Brutal King of the Ring'). Giant Haystacks, Greek George Pefanis, Adrian Street (British and European Light-heavyweight champion), Ian Gilmour (the 'Flying Scot'), Basil Riley (Irish Heavyweight champion), Henry Novak and Guy Viltard. From Zambia came John Chipeta, John Mwale (the 'Singing Wrestler'), Larry Old, Willie 'Tiger Boy' Nkandu, Tennison Phiri and Hugo Mulenga. Tennison Phiri hurled Frenchman Jack Karamel to the canvas in Lusaka in a tournament promoted by Nic Nichol.

The turning point in wrestling in Zambia was on 1 May 1970 when Power Mike, reputedly Africa's strongest man, and European Heavyweight champion Josef Kovacs staked their reputations in a duel fight in Kitwe. The *Zambia Mail*, the forerunner to the *Zambia Daily Mail*, reported that heated arguments raged in Kitwe and other Copperbelt towns, in Lusaka and Kabwe, as to just who of the slightly larger-than-life-he-men would triumph over the other. The paper said Power Mike and Kovacs might have felt something similar to the sentiments the old Roman gladiators were subjected to when entering the Colossium and say to the public: '*Morituri te salutumus*,' meaning 'We who are about to die salute you.' On street corners and across shop counters, over drinks in bars and hotels, the Power Mike/Josef Kovacs fight generated a lot of debate.

Kovacs, then thirty-eight years of age, began his wrestling career at the age of fourteen as an amateur while still at school. He clinched the World Amateur Heavyweight crown in 1954, turned professional in 1957 and won the European championship in 1961. He vowed he would retire if he lost to Power Mike.

The background story of Power Mike showed that he was twenty-eight years of age and reputedly the strongest man in Africa, who had stunned audiences in the United States of America and Europe with his Herculian feats. He started wrestling in Greece in 1968 and was clearly the favourite to beat Kovacs in the eyes of the Zambian Public.

As it turned out, Power Mike was disqualified in the fifth round by referee Fred Coates. He was also cautioned for clinging to his opponent's neck for far too long. Fred Coates, Zambia's Heavyweight champion, had earlier thrown out of the ring Barry Lindo to win by a knockout in the fourth round. Zambian John Chipeta performed brilliantly by drawing with Henry Novak at a pinfall each. Franco-African Guy Viltard defeated Blackie Hall on a technical knockout.

After retaining his heavyweight title against Lindo, Coates announced his retirement from the ring for what he termed 'business commitments and old age.' He also renounced his championship.

Fearless Coates began wrestling at the age of sixteen in South Africa and fought against the likes of Ski Lee, the 'Kalahari Wildman,' Zando Zabo, Quasa Modo, Josef Kovacs and many others. When he moved North in the mid-1920's Coates won, in succession, the Northern Rhodesia, Southern Rhodesia and Federal championships.

Eventually, after numerous pleas from his fans, Coates agreed to come out of retirement on 5 June 1970 to defend his honour in what was billed as a do-or-die bout against Power Mike at the Independence Stadium in Lusaka. During the build up to the fight Coates warned that if Power Mike tried to strangle him as he did against Kovacs, he would break off his fingers and throw them out of the ring one by one and that lifting motor engines did not make one a wrestler, to which Power Mike replied that he would not prepare for the fight because Coates 'was too small.' After a fierce contest the judges' ruling was a draw. The spectators on the other hand voted Coates the winner and lifted him shoulder high all the way to the dressing room to show their appreciation. Power Mike later apologized to the Zambian public for his disappointing showing in the fight saying that he did not apply his energy on Coates for Coates 'is an old man.' Had he defeated Coates in the first round the spectators would have gone away very disappointed.

As wrestling gained popularity, Gideon Lumpa, as acting Chairman of the Zambia Professional Boxing and Wrestling Control Board at the time suggested that the only way to keep wrestling alive was for the Zambians themselves to participate in the sport and not be mere spectators. Another way of boosting the sport would be to approach the Amateur Boxing Association of Zambia and ask them to incorporate wrestling into their programmes.

In 1973, when wrestling was still at its zenith, President Kenneth Kaunda commended wrestler Nicholas Chaya for offering scholarships tenable in Greece to Zambia wrestlers John Mwale and Hugo Mulenga. The President made the remarks when he bade farewell to four international wrestlers at a brief State House ceremony. The wrestlers were Man Jack, Masambula, King Kong and Power Mike who had been on a two-week tour of Zambia, with performances in Lusaka and the Copperbelt.

Wrestling, at that time, was well organized and second only to football as acrowd-puller. Through the medium of television, Zambians were able to monitor European and American wrestling. The country also enjoyed the cream of international wrestling through tournaments staged here. All this contributed to raising the standards locally.

Eventually, however, locall training facilities dwindled with the departure of several expatriates from the sport's administration. In July 1982 Chingola's Fisher Promotions promoted the last international tournament in the country which featured seven British wrestlers, namely Middleweight champion Brian Maxie, Heavy-middleweight champion Nick Michael, Marty

Jones, Pat Patton, Jack Turnpin, Heavy-middleweight Mick McManus and Middleweight Johnny England. This all-star tournament was a flop. 'It cost K35,000 to maintain the seven Britons on the Copperbelt and Lusaka from July 2 to 10,' promoter Fisher said.

BADMINTON

There is some doubt as regards the origin of the game of Badminton. Popular belief is that the game originated in India. It was played by English military officers in the early 1870's at Poona, a Western Indian city and was accordingly known as 'POONA.'

Popular belief is that the name Badminton was adopted by a group of English army officers, home on leave from India in 1873. Due to inclement weather they were forced to play the game inside the great Badminton Hall, the seat of the Duke of Beaufort in Gloucestershire, England. Badminton started initially as a lawn game but later on became an indoor sport to allow people to play the game thoughout the year, undisturbed by the vagaries of weather.

In the 1880's the game became popular in England and the Badminton Association of England (BAE) was born with fourteen registered clubs. Englishmen took the game overseas to their colonies as well as to the USA, and other countries in Europe. The long British tradition for Badminton is continued in the All England Championships staged every year since 1899 (excepting the war periods). Initially, British and Danish players dominated this annual event. In fact until 1977, the All England Championships were regarded as the unofficial world championships. Here players like the Indonesian Rudy Hartono – a record eight time singles champion between 1968-76, the Danish Erland Kops – seven times singles title winner from 1958 -67, and the American Judy Hashman (nee Delvin) - ten times women's title winner between 1954-66 – made themselves immortal.

The first international badminton competition, the Thomas Cup Championship, was inaugurated in 1948. The women's equivalent to the Thomas Cup was named Uber Cup Championships and was first played in

1956 when an American team emerged as the winners. Indonesia and China were the winners of the 1984 Thomas Cup and Uber Cup respectively.

In 1934 the International Badminton Federation was founded with the national organizations of fifteen countries. The People's Republic of China was not a member of the IBF until 1979, although Chinese players were known to be among the best in the world. Seventeen Asian and African countries withdrew from the IBF in 1977 over the issue of the inclusion of Taiwan and that of undemocratic voting system. In the same year, the People's Republic of China, along with these seventeen nations, formed a parallel world Badminton body and named it the World Badminton Federation (W.B.F). However, in 1980, the two organizations decided to bury the hatched and unify.

The year 1979 was a landmark in the history of badminton. This was the year that badminton had decided to go 'open' by allowing licenced players to accept prize money and advertisement money. For the licenced players a system of points based on their performance was devised and in December every year the top twelve played the Grand Prix Finals. Morten Frost of Denmark and Han Aipeng of China won the Men's and Women's events in 1984.

The leisurely game of lawn badminton had come a long way to become one of the toughest in the world of sport, needing razor-blade sharp reflexes, movements like a ballet dancer and stamina like a horse to be one among those at the top.

Lastly, towards the end of a tiring and entertaining day of badminton, let us spare a moment's thought for the millions of geese that have been sacrificed to make shuttlecocks. The tiny five grams shuttle is made from the feathers selected from three geese. Consequently, the expensive feather shuttlecocks which are still used in all international tournaments are slowly but surely being replaced by less expensive and longer lasting nylon shuttlecocks.

Zambia was affiliated to the International Badminton Federation in 1948- then known as the Northern Rhodesia Badminton Association. This affiliation lasted until 1952 when Northern Rhodesia resigned and joined the South African Badminton Union until Independence, when Zambia was re-affiliated to the International Badminton Federation. The IBF was then headed by Erik Nielsen as president.

Badminton is a very popular sport in secondary schools, largely along the line of rail and some provincial centres where school halls are available for use. In the early days, badminton in schools flourished, particularly on the Copperbelt, thanks to Sean Gallagher, who was instrumental for the Christine Nyahoda fame. Nyahoda, then attending Ibenga Girls Secondary School near Luanshya, was the national women's singles champion for many years. Other notable players were Naomi Shamatutu, Theresa Koloko, Louisa

Mukangwa and others who etched themselves international fame through the enthusiasm of Gallagher, a geography teacher and sportsmaster who organized tours to West Germany, Denmark and England in 1975.

Nyahoda won the Zambia Closed singles title and doubles with Theresa Koloko several times during the period 1975-80. Among this group was Louisa Mukangwa who was studying for her 'A' levels at Bath Technical College in Britain, and who was invited to join the group in Frankfurt, West Germany. Born and brought up in Luanshya, Louisa began playing badminton in the third term of Form Three (Grade Ten) in 1971 and has been playing ever since. Mukangwa said, 'Out of a group of girls who began playing badminton (mostly my classmates), five of us – Angela Chilando, Maggie Chinyama, Annette Nkamba, Olga Mundonga and myself played in various tournaments during 1972/73.'

During this period Louisa won the Copperbelt Open, Copperbelt Closed (twice), the Midlands Open and the Zambia women's singles titles. In the doubles tournaments, Mukangwa and her partner Annette Nkamba won the Zambia Closed, Copperbelt Open and the Copperbelt Closed doubles titles. Mukangwa added, 'Sean Gallagher was our driving force behind all the success.'

Following in the footsteps were junior players such as Christine Nyahoda, Theresa Koloko, Anne Machupa and Louisa Mukangwa's younger sister, Mary. Christine Nyahoda was voted Sportswoman of the Year in 1977 - an award sponsored by Rothmans of Pall Mall Zambia Limited. Not only did the Zambian female players achieve international fame, but the men as well, with names such as Vish Kapil and Ajit Tikekar standing out. The badminton league both on the Copperbelt and in the Midlands was actively contested by the various clubs. The annual Copperbelt versus the Midlands duel sponsored by Leopold Walford Limited was the highlight of the year in Zambia.

In 1977 Zambia was instrumental in the formation of the African Badminton Federation with Vish Kapil as its vice-president. Unfortunately Zambia did not participate in the first African championships held in Ghana. Due to an administration mix up, the team consisting of two top juniors Charles Chimata and Bernard Mwape, arrived in Accra while the tournament was being played in Kumasi! Zambia nevertheless sent a junior side to the next championship held in Mozambique in June 1980 comprising Shailesh Patel, Nicholas Kaoma and Madhavi Tijoriwala, who did Zambia proud by reaching the finals. Madhavi Tijoriwala was the 1982 Sportswoman of the Year and left an almost impeccable record on the Zambian badminton map.

A short lull in badminton activities occurred in 1980 due to the stepping down of the administration. However, an enthusiastic steering Committee headed by Andrew Kashita was formed in 1981, after the Midlands Badminton

Board took the initiative through its Chairman, Hiran Ray. More and more indigenous Zambians were infused into the cream of badminton society of Zambia.

Zambia again participated in the Third African Championships held in Lagos, Nigeria in May 1982. Included in this team was Simon Gondwe, who displayed exceptional ability against a strong opposition in the Nigerians as well as an unfavourable hot and humid climate. Zambia won a silver medal. Other players in the team were Mike Wilmott, Hiran Ray, Raj Patel, Madhavi Tijoriwala, Shailesh Patel and Ajay Misra.

Zambia hosted the Zambia Open in 1982 at which Mukesh Shah of Tanzania proved a little too much for our Simon Gondwe in the finals.

In the same year a team from the Midlands was invited to participate in the Independence Day celebrations of Zimbabwe in Harare. The team under the leadership of Hiran Ray, comprised players like Mike Wilmott, a powerhouse on the domestic scene, Raj Patel, Ajay Misra, Priscilla Mutambirwa, Joan Dennis and Madhavi Tijoriwala. Out of the five team matches, Zambia beat four provinces and was beaten only once.

In the month of December 1982, the Midlands Badminton Association, initiated a triangular badminton tournament to be participated in by teams from the Midlands, the Copperbelt and Mashonaland (Zimbabwe). The Midlands with players like Madhavi Tijoriwala, Priscilla Mutambirwa and Shailesh Patel, won all the matches and the trophy donated by City TV Hire of Lusaka.

1983 was not such a good year for badminton in Zambia due to a terrible shortage of shuttlecocks, resulting in the suspension of both leagues with only the regional Closed and the Copperbelt Open being played. Many of the people who had helped to keep badminton going in the country left and enthusiasm declined.

Zambia's first participation in the Men's World Team Event – the Thomas Cup – was in 1984. Zambia sent its team to Ostend, Belgium, comprising Hiran Ray (manager), Arnold Nyirenda (official), Bernard Mwape, Ramesh Patel, Bernard Chimfwembe, Jerry Kalulu, Simon Gondwe and Majority Chola. Athough they could not hope to qualify for the finals against players from all over the world, the experience gained was invaluable and proved fruitful in due course. During 1984 a leadership wrangle developed between the Zambia Badminton Association and the Copperbelt Badminton Association which was not resolved until May 1985. Regional tournaments were held with household names such as Madhavi Tijoriwala, Mike Wilmott, Simon Gondwe, Joan Dennis, Hiran Ray and Ramesh Patel bagging the available titles.

The fourth All-Africa Championships were held in August 1984 in Dar-es-Salaam, Tanzania. Zambia participated and again played second fiddle to Tanzania in most matches, but Simon Gondwe brought home the Africa Men's Singles Trophy after a scintillating final against Feroz of Tanzania.

1985 brought in a fresh consignment of equipment such as shoes, rackets, strings and shuttlecocks and the game picked up, so much that new clubs were formed both on the Copperbelt and in the Midlands. Prominent players Simon Gondwe, Abraham Mutale, Josephine Chipepo, Catherine Chisala, Aquinata Moya, Rogers Chilufya, could all be found playing in one final or another in the tournaments they participate in. Some of the promising Midlands players like Catherine Chisala, Josephine Chipepo and Abraham Mutale have been coached by Hiran Ray.

1986 proved another turning point in Zambia badminton, with the participation in the International Badminton Federation Thomas Cup for men and the Uber Cup for women held in Mulheim, West Germany. In the Thomas Cup Zambia was placed in Group B against Sweden, Austria, France and Iceland. The Zambian women also played in Group B against Scotland, Austria, Switzerland and Sweden and for the Uber Cup. Aquinata Moya and Majority Chola were outstanding and gave their opponents some fine games.

More participation of this nature in internationally contested tournaments can only help Zambian badminton steer ahead to greater heights. The continued good supply of equipment, a sound administration and enough sponsorship to keep the clubs going will ensure Zambia's rise on this continent and in time on a world perspective.

Dr de Silva, former singles champion of Sri Lanka, who was an employee of Zambia Consolidated Copper Mines (ZCCM), took over from where Sean Gallagher left off. He was instrumental in raising players like Simon Gondwe, Rogers Chilufya, Bernard Chimfwembe and Ben Mwape.

Some of the notable players were:

Sailesh Patel: Midlands Closed Champion 1983/4, selected to represent Zambia for the third and fourth All-Africa Badminton Championships in Lagos (1982) and Dar-es-Salam (1984) respectively. Also selected to represent the Zambian junior team for the Junior World Badminton Tournament in Mozambique (1982). Studied in the United States of America.

Ajay Misra: Former schoolboy champion. Represented Zambia at the third All-Africa Badminton Championships in Lagos and also participated in the Junior World Badminton Championships in Mozambique. Studied in the United States of America.

Ramesh Patel: Represented Zambia at the Thomas World Cup Badminton Tournament in Ostend, Belgium, (1984 and the fourth All-Africa Badminton Championships in Dar-es-Saalam. Also won the Zambia Open Men's Doubles title in 1982 partnered with Sallesh Patel.

Simon Gondwe: All-Africa badminton singles title holder. He played for Chibuluma Mine Club. He represented Zambia in the third and fourth all-Africa Championships. He was the Zambia Closed champion.

Catherine Chisala: She played for Lusaka Central Sports Club and was the Midlands Closed singles title holder. She was ranked No. 3 in the country.

Josephine Chipepo: Also from Lusaka Central Sports Club. An excellent doubles Player and was the Midlands women's doubles title holder in partnership with Catherine Chisala. Represented Zambia in the Uber Cup Competition in 1986 in Mulheim, West Germany.

Aquinata Moya: Zambia Closed singles title holder from the Copperbelt. Also won the title in 1985. Has represented Zambia in the Uber Cup Competition in Mulheim, West Germany in 1986.

Figure 30: Flashback: A smiling champion receiving her award at ceremony as guest of honour and Copperbelt Province Minister Shadrack Soko looks on.

BOXING

The most significant achievement recorded immediately after attaining Independence in 1964 in boxing in Zambia was the unification of the former European amateur Boxing Association and the former African Amateur Boxing Association to form the Amateur Boxing Association of Zambia.

As early as 1965, Zambia played host to Uganda in a friendly tournament which took place in Chingola. Nchanga A.B.C. was one of the well organized clubs in the country and the men behind this organization were Gideon Lumpa, Bill Land and Simon Chikwavaire. Zambia featured well in the tournament with Julius Luipa winning his fight.

In 1965 Zambia sent three boxers for the All-Africa Games in Congo Brazzaville. Only Jackson Mambwe won a Bronze medal.

In 1968 Zambian boxing was exposed to a major international competition when it hosted the Fourth All-Africa Amateur Boxing Championships in Lusaka at the Showgrounds. This was a well attended tournament. The World president of the International Amateur Boxing Association (IABA) Colonel Russel, Australian boxing president John Castle, Pakistani boxing president professor Coudry, Karl Magrabi (who was chairman of the Referees and Judges Commission), M. Houshi, president of the Africa Amateur Boxing Association, Godfrey Amatifio, one of the first African IABA judges/referees from Ghana, Kid Bassey, Roy Ankara, to mention but a few, all attended the Championship.

Zambia fielded eight boxers. These were David Natta (flyweight), Kenny Mwansa (flyweight), Godfrey Mwamba, Hobley Chisenga (bantamweight), Hugo Chansa (featherweight), Julius Luipa (welterweight), Son Mwila (light-heavyweight) and Mark Sampa (heavyweight). Egypt won the Championships, but Zambia managed to win three medals, one Silver medal by Julius Luipa and two bronze medals by Kenny Mwansa and Son Mwila. The same year in

December, Zambia competed in the Mexico Olympics and was eliminated in the preliminaries.

In May 1972 Zambia invited the Kenya, Swaziland and Zaire Boxing Associations. Zambia beat Kenya in Lusaka in a return match. In Kitwe Zambia beat Swaziland and Kenya during the Kitwe Agricultural Show. Lottie Mwale fought David Allan, a Kenyan bronze medalist in the 1970 Commonwealth Games. The Zairean team was pitched against the Zambia B team, which consisted mainly of Copperbelt boxers.

When the news of the Olympic Games to be staged in West Germany was received, there was confusion as to Africa's participation in these Games. The decision on South Africa was reached only two days before the start of the boxing competition while the Zambian boxers were still in Zambia. They eventually arrived in Munich with some being overweight. Others could not adjust to the German weather. As a result all the Zambian boxers lost in the preliminary rounds.

In 1973 Zambia participated in the All-Africa Games which took place in Lagos, Nigeria. Timothy Feruka was selected to represent Africa in the Latin American Games in the flyweight division after he had won a gold medal. The African boxing team to the Latin American Games comprised the following:

Light Flyweight	James Odouri (Uganda)
Flyweight	Timothy Feruka (Zambia)
Bantamweight	A. Habibu (Tanzania)
Featherweight	G. Oduori (Kenya)
Lightweight	Ibrahim Howard (Sudan)
Light Welterweight	Obisia Nwankpa (Nigeria)
Welterweight	Bella Barry (Guinea-Conakry)
Middleweight	Peter Dula (Kenya)
Light Middleweight	Myeri Mohammed (Tunisia)
Light Heavyweight	I. Ikhuoria (Nigeria)
Heavyweight	F. Ahinla (Nigeria)

Latin America won the competition by seven bouts to four. The four African winners were led by Timothy Feruka, who won 4-1, Obisia Nwankpa 3-2, Peter Dula R.S.C. in the third round, and Fatai Ahinla R.S.C. in the first round. The African team was coached by Hogan Kid Bassey of Nigeria from 20 July to 7 August, 1973.

In 1969 Bill Chanda led a team of seven boxers to Uganda. Of the seven boxers, only Hugo Chansa won his fight. The rest lost. In December 1969 Zambia was invited by Kenya Amateur Boxing Association to participate in the country's Independence celebrations. Eight boxers travelled to Kenya. Zambia lost narrowly to Kenya, but it was the opposite when Kenya came to Zambia in May 1970 during Zambia's preparations for the Commonwealth Games, which took place in Edinburgh, Scotland, Zambia beat Kenya at Lusaka's Showgrounds. Kenya was beaten again in Chingola. The most sensational bout was that of Julius Luipa against Stephen Tega. The two boxers fought twice in Lusaka and in Chingola, and Luipa won both fights.

After the Kenya tour a Zambian team went to Uganda in June 1970. This time the venue was not Kampala but Kilembe. The eight Zambians who travelled won three bouts and lost five. Those who won their bouts were Julius Luipa with a knock-out in the second round, Leo Mwansa on points and Billy Soose with a knock-out in the third round.

At the 1970 Edinburgh Games nine boxers competed. This was the largest boxing team to be entered by Zambia in any international competition. Bill Chanda was then vice-president of the Amateur Boxing Association of Zambia and coach. The team was prepared by Allan Wilson and Enock Ndu Eneke before Chanda took over. It consisted of the following boxers:

Light Welterweight	Blackson Mazyopa
Flyweight	David Natta (late)
Bantamweight	Arnold Katakala
Featherweight	Godfrey Mwamba
Light Welterweight	Leo Mwansa
Light Welterweight	Hugo Chansa (late)
Welterweight	Paul Mulenga
Light Middleweight	Julius Luipa
Middleweight	Billy Soose (Samuel Kasongo)

Some Amateur Boxing Association of Zambia officials had gone ahead to Scotland to cheer the team and these consisted of Bob Blandford, then president ot ABAZ, Davie Angel, general secretary and Alister Robertson, chairman of Lusaka ABC.

On departure, Chanda predicted a harvest of four medals, but Zambia won one silver through Julius Luipa and two bronze through Paul Mulenga and Billy Soose. Julius Luipa was openly robbed of the Gold medal.

In December the same year Zambia was invited by Kenya Amateur Boxing Association to take part in a tournament during that country's Independence celebrations. The competitions were held in Nairobi and Nakuru. Zambia lost narrowly in Nairobi but won the Nakurru tournament. The same trip was extended to Tanzania where the Zambians hammered the hosts.

In May 1971, Bill Chanda, the ABAZ chairman led a team to the first

East and Central African Federation Boxing Championships held in Kenya at the Nairobi City Hall. This team included Lottie Mwale, who was only sixteen years of age and Timothy Feruka. Mwale was a welterweight and Feruka was the new national light-flyweight champion. Zambia had problems in the heavier divisions.

During this encounter, Funwell Mwanza, popularly known as 'Blow Top' was a light-heavyweight boxer. On arrival in Kenya, the Zambian delegation discovered that there were only two heavyweight boxers from Kenya and Uganda. Chanda then decided to elevate 'Blow Top' to the heavyweight division by encouraging him to have a heavy breakfast, with lots of Coca-Cola. This brought his weight up to over eight-one kilogrammes. When the draws were made Zambia had a bye and thus qualified to the finals. In the semi finals of heavyweight division contest, Uganda beat Kenya. The finals were then between Zambia and Uganda. Before the end of the contest Chanda was recalled home to attend UNIP General Conference. On the day of the finals a Ugandan doctor who examined all the boxers disqualified Funwell Mwanza on the grounds of septic wound on his right leg. The Ugandan boxer, therefore, got the gold medal. Mwanza who never threw a punch throughout the Championships got the Silver.

It was at this tournament that Lottie Mwale's talent was tapped. Mwale fought a very experienced Ugandan boxer, Davie Jackson. It was a tough fight but Mwale lost on a split points decision in the semi finals. Kenya were the winners whilst Zambia and Uganda drew for second place.

In 1974 Zambia was at the Commonwealth Games in Auckland, New Zealand. Zambia registered the first gold medal through Lottie Mwale. History was made. Zambia also participated in the Federation of East and Central African Amateur Boxing Associations (FECABA) Championships in Tanzania, the winners being Kenya, Zambia hosted the fifth FECABA Cfhampionships which she won.

In the 1976 Montreal Olympic games Zambia had an even chance to win her first Olympic medal through Lottie Mwale. Mwale was in good shape and was drawn against Michael Spinks of the United States of America. However, the Games witnessed an Afro-Arab withdrawal and that put paid to Zambia's chances.

Zambia participated in the 1980 Moscow Olympics. The Games were boycotted by the United States of America and its allies over the Afghanistan issue. However, a mini-Olympic Games boxing competition was staged by Kenya in December where Zambia featured extremely well – Gold, Silver and Bronze medals being won.

1n 1981 Zambia hosted the FECABA Championships. Zimbabwe

was admitted to the membership of the Federation and did extremely well. However, Zambia were the overall winners in these Championships.

In 1982 Zambia took part in the Commonwealth Games in Brisbane, Australia. She won a Silver and five Bronze medals. The Silver was attained through Lackson Mukobe. Zambia also participated in the FECABA championships in Zimbabwe and emerged runners-up to Kenya.

1n 1983 Ethiopia hosted the FECABA Championships. The countries participating included Kenya, Uganda, Swaziland, Zambia, Zimbabwe and the host country.

Zambia emerged winners, with Kenya second and Uganda third. Zambia was invited by Kenya for a three-nation tournament in which she faired well. Uganda hosted the All-Africa amateur Boxing Championshis which were won by, with Zambia in second place. Participating countries included Nigeria, Ghana, Cameroun, Algeria, Tunisia and all the active members of the FECABA.

In 1984, prior to the Olympics hosted by the United States of America, the USA offered to help Zambia in her preparation for the Olympics proper and also provided Coaches for this purpose. A pre-Olympic warm-up was held against Kenya in Zambia. Kenya emerged winners of both tournaments in Lusaka and Kafue. Zambia sent a team to Malawi to participate in two tournaments – in Lilongwe and in Blantyre. Zambia emerged winners of both tournaments.

The contingent of Zambian boxers to the 1984 Olympics comprised Keith 'Spinks' Mwila, Patrick Chisanga Mwaba, Star Zulu, Chris Mwamba, Jaineck Chinyata, Dimas Chisala, Henry Kalunga, the late Chris Kapopo and Moses Mwaba, making a total of nine. Zambia was awarded a bronze medal through southpaw Mwila, making this the first medal ever won by Zambia in the Olympics. If the judges had been fair, Mwila would have won the Gold.

In a further effort to popularize boxing in Zambia, various competitions were introduced. These included the Champion of Champions sponsored by the Zambia Agricultural and Commercial Show Society.

In 1985 Amateur Boxing Association of Zambia fixtures began with the Champion of Champions for which the Zambia National Building Society donated K29,000. Zambia also participated in the FECABA Championships, coming second to Kenya. The ABAZ took part in the Germany Democratic Republic (GDR) competitions which lasted two weeks and thereafter in the sixteenth GDR International competitions.

Zambia besides its national team, has a Defence boxing team. This team has participated and won regional, African and world championships. The largest haul of medals was achieved in the 1985 Zimbabwe Regional Military championships in which Zambia won nine Gold out of the twelve at stake.

Zambia is a boxing country. Clubs are run on a part-time basis. The National Executive is also on a part-time basis. Funds were raised from weekly tournaments at club level of a 10 percent levy on gate takings and also from Inter-Provincial tournaments. The ABAZ also received donations from the various sectors of the economy and sponsors. An annual grant of K2,000 from the then Ministry of Youth and Sport was a regular feature as was the K2,000 that was donated by BP Zambia Building Society broke a record in 1985 when they sponsored the filming of the Champion of Champions television series with a donation of K29,000.

The Zambia Agricultural and Commercial Show Society has also sponsored the Inter-Provincial Championships from 1981-84 at K4,000 a year and in 1985 this was increased to K5,000.

The major problem the Amateur Boxing Association of Zambia has been facing in its efforts to develop and promote boxing in the country has been finance. But the overriding problem has been lack of equipment. Some clubs may have the money but the equipment is not available. These comprise training and tournament gloves, punch bags, medicine balls, speedballs and mitts. Also as a result of financial problems, the Association has not been able to pay for the Amateur International Boxing Association (AIBA) courses for judges and referees to enable Zambians qualify as referees and judges at the Olympics, Commonwealth Games and World championships. It has slowed the pace of the Coaches' training programme.

One of the men who have done a lot for Zambian amateur boxing is former ABAZ chairman, Bill Chanda. Chanda was associated with the sport since 1954 – both as a boxer and an administrator. He turned to the administration of boxing in 1965 when he became chairman of Chililabombwe ABC.

During the preparations for the Fourth All-Africa Amateur Boxing Championships (1966-68) which were held at Chilililabombwe ABC with Chanda as chairman, most of the money was raised through the sales of raffle tickets. Chanda was appointed Public Relations Officer for the Championships. He qualified as a Judge in April and a Referee in December 1967. In 1969 Chanda was the first African to be elected vice-president. In August 1970 Chanda became the first indigenous Zambian kpresident of the Amateur Boxing Association of Zambia. During his reign as president/chairman the following reforms and medals were introduced/won:

- Weekly tournaments from club invitations and monthly tournaments

- Provincial zones

- Inter-Provincial tournaments

- 1970: three medals won at the Edinburgh Commonwealth Games

- 1971: medals won at the first FECABA Championshis, Nairobi, Kenya

- 1973: medals won at the Lagos All-Africa Games and Latin American Games

- 1974: Lottie Mwale won Zambia's first Gold medal at the Auckland Commonwealth Games in New Zealand and other boxers won Silver and Bronze

- 1975: medals won at FECABA Championships in Lusaka

- 1981: medals won at FECABA Championships in Lusaka

- 1982: medals won at the Brisbane Commonwealth Games in Australia and the Zimbabwe FECABA Championships

- 1983: medals won at the Ethiopian championship and Uganda All-Africa Amateur Boxing Championshios

- 1984: first Bronze medal won at the Los Angeles Olympic Games, United States of America

- 1985: medals on at the FECABA Championships in Nairobi, Kenya, and the Military boxing team won nine Gold medals at the Zimbabwe Regional Championships

Other present and past notable administrators in the field of boxing include Ernest Mate, Isaac Phiri, Captain Peter Mulenga, Mathew Ponga, Archie Phiri, Godfrey Munalula, Vincent Mudenda, John Shula, Andrew Lubesha and Pady Linnane. The ABAZ executive was headed by Chairman Colonel Panji Kaunda.

Zambia amateur boxing has had some joyous moments in the winning of the medals at various tournaments, particularly Gold ones. There have also been sad moments due to the deaths of various personalities such as Peter Mulenga of Nchanga A.B.C., Eddie Malama of Mufulira A.B.C., Hugo Chansa of Rokana A.B.C., David Natta of Rokana A.B.C., Ulbano Mutale of Tug-Argan A.B.C., Max Katongo of Kabwe A.B.C., and administrator Sichande of Nchanga A.B.C., and national coach Archie Phiri.

Past Champions include Patrick Mambwe, Jackson Mambwe, John Musonda, David Natta, Arnold Katakala, Julius Luipa, Timothy Feruka, Francis Musankabala, Dominic Musankabala, elder brother of Francis and Albert, Paul Mulenga, Lottie Mwale, Billy Soose and Laston Mukobe. From this record one can conclude that amateur boxing in Zambia has grown and standards have risen tremendously in the past twenty-four years.

Profesional Boxing

As far back as 1967 the Rokana A.B.C. housed in the O.B. Bennet Hall catered for the training of professional boxers. They, however, did not feature in any tournaments.

The sport began to pick up when some of the outstanding amateurs switched to the paid ranks. These young men were evidently a better quality of boxers. For instance, the late Hugo Chansa easily grabbed the title from the much feared 'Lion of Kitwe' Lemmy Chipili in 1972. Chansa tamed the 'Lion' in a third round knockout. Chansa also had it easy against George Chisenga, who had a powerful punch and a combination similar to David Natta's. Sadly, Chansa died after being knocked out in the fifth round by Don McMillan, a strong Scotsman, in a Pius Kakungu promotion in Kitwe's Rokana Club. The fight was refereed by Paddy Linnane, a former Amateur Boxing Association of Zambia official and organizing secretary of the 1968 first All-Africa Boxing Championships. David Natta, Chansa's long time friend said, 'when Hugo got up from the canvas he said he felt dizzy and confused.'

After winning a silver medal in the 1970 Commonwealth Games, David Natta turned professional and dethroned Patrick Mambwe in a third round knockout. Mambwe had his revenge in 1972 when he regained his title with a stoppage in the seventh round. Joe Dytch, Mambwe's former Coach, returned from South Africa to help the boxer in the training for the rematch. He instructed Mambwe to pray for time as Natta was still fresh from a three round session. His advice apparently worked.

Natta was also Zambia's third boxing export, the first being Leonard Masaiti, alias 'Kid Miller,' and the second being Patrick Mambwe. Natta later returned from abroad with a detatched retina and as a result his boxing licence was withdrawn on medical grounds. Still budding with talent though, Natta broke both medical rules and national policy on sporting links with apartheid south Africa by fighting in South Africa on two occasions. He also flew to Australia, but the Australian Boxing Board of Control could not clear him for the fight without Zambian clearance. He returned home a demoralized man and this marked the end of his career. He died on 22 December 1982 in Kitwe Central Hospital. He was aged 32.

Natta had a illustrious professional boxing career. The fights with Patrick Mambwe were epic stuff – his amateur career was also excellent.

Natta fought in the Mexico Olympics in Mexico where he lost in the qualifying rounds in 1968. Two years later he was outpointed by

David Needham of Britain in a flyweight qualifying rounds bout of the Commonwealth Games in Scotland. He turned professional and moved into the bantamweight division where he soon took the title. But he did not hold the title for too long as Mambwe dethroned him in a fight in Kitwe in 1971.

In 1972 Natta left for Italy where he was managed by Marcellis of Desportive Stables. He returned to Zambia in 1973. In March 1974 Natta's professional career was dealt a blow when the Zambian Professional Wrestling and Boxing Board of Control revoked his licence shortly before his fight against John McLuskey of Britain in Lusaka because he was found medically unfit. After examining Natta, the board discovered that he had a detached retina in the left eye, an injury he sustained in Italy. Months later, the board barred Natta from fighting Victor Mwaba in Luanshya in an eliminatory contest for the national bantamweight title.

Yotham Kunda was yet another Zambian boxing 'export' to Europe. On his return home he easily beat Isaac Jacobs of Ndola at Nakatindi Hall in Lusaka and compatriot Flos Chinyanta to become Zambian welterweight champion, a title he later lost to Payson Choolwe.

Paul Mulenga made a brief appearance in the professional ranks, which included beating two Malawians when promoter Gibson Nwosu opened a link with that country.

Julius Luipa, the 1970 Commonwealth Games silver medalist, turned professional and beat George Chisenga to grab the light heavyweight title. But his reign was shortlived for Lottie Mwale, the man he allegedly avoided in the amateur ranks turned professional and subsequently took the title away from him after beating 'King Blow Top' Funwell Mwanza in a warm up fight. When Mwale shuffled and ducked in the ring erected in the centre of a playing field in Lusaka, thousands of men, women and children shrieked, swayed and lept to the rhythm of his incomparable right craft. They were never tired of watching this dazzling man as, every time he was in action, they trooped to the venue to jam the seats in the stands and ringside, or stand shoulder to shoulder to the leeward side of a nearby hill if they could not afford the gate charges to marvel over the fighting prowess of Lottie Gunduzani Mwale, the 'Leopard' of the boxing ring considered the best light-heavyweight ever in local boxing circles and indeed the best boxer ever produced by the country. Mwale was credited for setting the standards of professional boxing in Zambia. His classic fights will forever remain engraved on the minds of many Zambian boxing fans.

At the peak of his career, Mwale almost single-handedly managed to elevate boxing above all other national sports. The popularity which the sport assumed when Mwale brought home both the African and the

Commonwealth light-heavyweight titles within the first five years of his entering the professional ranks in 1977 was so overwhelming that the crowds which gathered to witness his contests by far surpassed those recorded at international football matches.

The enigmatic aura that emanated from Mwale's being was all due to the fact that he was the only boxer in the country capable of fighting with intelligence, clean style and strength, usually knocking out his opponents. The captivating style was not that he danced and fluttered his wings in the ring as most so-called 'flashy' boxers want to do, Mwale's was a sure-footed amble, the picturesque grace which set the opponents in a state of nerves as they bounced around him in great acts of showmanship. The psychological trap in this was that the opponents gathered false confidence from their apparent flexibility as opposed to Mwale's rooted stance. Their mobility however, rendered them vulnerable to Mwale's sudden spurts of attack which almost always caught them on the wrong foot. They fell without staggering.

Without much variation, the somersaults on the canvass marked the beginning of a long, oblivious trip back to consciousness, always tenable at the University Teaching Hospital's (UTH) emergency ward, a 10-minute full-speed ambulance ride into the heart of Lusaka.

The stage-man's proclamations about who the winner was and in what round of the contest was whatever the definition of the ending was often redundant as the myriad of overstretched throats went hoarse with the common chant of Lottie! Lottie! In the ensuing din, the crackling sound of the microphone was just an addition to the noisy pandemonium.

Who would need to be told anyway, when it was so obvious with the opponent still lying sprawled and cold on the the canvass that Gunduzani (shake it/him) had lived up to his name again? Certainly not the all knowing disciples.

The local press dubbed Mwale's fist the Nuclear Power-Packed Punch (NPPP) and as would be expected, the apt tag contaminated the tongues of fans like a plague. NPPP became a household name.

From far and wide, opponents flew in to stagger and crumble at the discretion of the NPPP. All Europe, All-Africa and part of America came under the guise of names such as Bob Smith, Lonnie Bennett, Garry Summerhays, Ba (Bagayuko) Sounkalo and Luis Pergaud. Their entrances were heralded by a storm of words that shook the streets of Lusaka, sweeping descriptions of all that they would do to Mwale in their pending encounters. Anxious crowds flocked to the venues looking uniformly solemn, their knees wobbly with the common fear of what they should expect to remain of their idol after these opponents were through with him. What they had heard and seen in newspapers sent chills of uncertainty up their spines. 'Will he manage this time?' they wondered.

Such was the anxiety with every different opponent that all openings of the brawls at Independence Stadium were marked by an ominous, almost eerie silence as the two adversaries exchanged jabs testily in the ring, sizing each other up.

The faithful home crowd got so adept at reading Mwale that from those few playful taps and shuffles in the first round, they could tell whether the fight would be lengthy and tough or brief and easy. But whatever the duration, the end was always the same – orgasmic chaos, explosive but both exciting and relieving.

Mwale was never the one to open his mouth unnecessarily, especially before a fight. He talked with his gloves, shutting up the opponents so that they departed in a pathetic state of aching bones and swollen tissues to go and sing a common song of defeat abroad.

His attitude in the ring earned Mwale yet another name which eventually came to be eblazoned on his pairs of fighting shorts – Kaingo, a Nyanja word for 'leopard.' Like a Kaingo, he moved stealthily around the canvass, and when he attacked it was with lightning speed and with such force that if the opponent did not backle at the knees, he would be so dazed that, he would wonder around the ring like a man in a trance.

Bless the poor man that the bell should sound, for if it did not then let him say amen.

Sounkalo once said the sun would not rise in Bamako if he was beaten to the African Boxing Union (ABU) light-heavyweight title which he wore to Lusaka for the long-awaited confrontation with the local cool-cat. But the poor man with a reach so long that his hands almost touched the ground while standing erect was to pitifully discover that he possessed no such divine powers over the solar system as the sun still smiled over the Malian capital despite his having been splendidly mauled in that fateful brawl at the Independence Stadium. After a disappointingly brief appearance in the ring- Sounkalo flew back to Bamako an ex-champion.

Away from home Mwale dazzled both fans and foes inside and outside the ring in such victories as the ones scored over stable-mate Bunny Johnson, John Conteh and Tony Sibson.

Riding on the dual championship mantle, the rumbling Zambian Kaingo was evidently ready for the ultimate in all boxing ambitions for the World championship.

With a clean record of twenty-one wins in as many fights over a three year professional experience, Mwale packed his kit and, under the auspices of George Francis' Wellington Stables in London, went to wage war against the then reigning World Boxing Council (WBC) light-heavyweight king, Mathew Saad Muhammad, of the United States of America in San Diego.

Passionate fanatics of boxing in the gambling city flocked to the venue to see this African marvel who had guts enough to dare try taint American supremacy in the sport, and against such an opponent as Saad with all his muscles of steel. Oh! What cunning humanity.

Turning up to the fight, Mwale even had a display bout with the world's greatest boxing hero, former heavyweight champion Muhammad Ali, who retired from the ring after a third come-back attempt foiled by emergent champion, Larry Holmes, also of the USA. Ali spoke well of Mwale after the bout, very promising news to the fans at home.

Mwale was made to taste his own medicine. The canvas to which he had so often sent others sprawling now and then again, had been his to lay his back on after a Saad block-buster in the fourth round of the contest. The nation was quiet. If anybody talked about the incident, it was in terse phrases that clearly said the subject would rather be left buried. It was mourning period and the people wiped their tears silently.

It was not the end of the world, they said, there was always a next time. Quietly, Mwale came back to gather his bones, cautiously regaining the confidence of his followers with two compensatory victories against Louise Pergaud of Cameroun and American Don Addison in 1981.

All this while, a local rival Chisanda Mutti had been gathering up confidence as an upcoming challenger, capable of nudging Mwale off the limelight. Capitalising on Mwale's poor show in America – the Mutti camp rallied up so much support that an encounter between the two former sparring partners was inevitable. Having risen considerably in Commonwealth ratings Mutti eventually challenged Mwale to the tittle in 1982 and put up such a spirited fight that he survived twelve rounds of the contest before succumbing in the thirteenth. So Mwale had a rival even at home!

So it was then that for sometime after the clash with Mutti, Mwale reinstated in the local public's minds the fact that he and only he was the greatest fighter in the republic. And these few encounters having improved his standing in world ratings, Mwale again set off for the land of boxing kings (USA) to tackle yet another tough boxer, Mustafa Muhammad (Eddie Gregory), who had impressive background. Mustafa Muhammad would be Mwale's last hurdle before he could have another attempt at the elusive WBC crown.

Two defeats in two years much credit to a fighter who hoped to remain respected by fans and foes alike. This surely was not the Lottie that had made the dust rise at Independence Stadium, the Lottie that had made tears well up in the eyes of opponents in shame and those of fans in awe.

Little heard-of-boxers even dared throw up challenges at the previously shirked Kaingo and they trickled in behind such names ad Kid Power from Zimbabwe, Mustapha Wasajja from Uganda and Len Welburn from the USA. These he beat at leisure, but Mutti could not be convinced until he had another go. He was also shipped amid a sizzling dispute over the scoring of points. He lasted the distance though!

Something was terribly wrong with Zambia's boxing idol as he slowly lost grip with his fans. They did not get what they wanted from him.

Where was the flair that drew multitudes, the charisma that made people to utter the name 'Lottie' with such reverent taste, savouring it the way one would to a bar of chocolate? How come these same boxers who previously flinched inwardly at the mention of Mwale came literally running to have a go at him?

It came like a joke therefore that an unheard of youth from the West Indies was challenging Mwale to the Commonwealth title. Leslie Stewart, of Trinidad and Tobago, was making a move that three years previously, would have been flippantly dismissed with a chuckle as it would have been considered suicidal. But there he was, in 1985, beckoning Mwale to take his entire person of a champion to that island for the fight.

And for sure, he outpointed the Zambian in a full distance contest in Port-of Spain and Mwale came back crownless. Stewart went on to win the WBC champion the following year while Mwale was again beaten to the African Boxing Union (ABU) title by a Nigerian Joe Lasisi in April 1986.

Such a humiliating experience was surely more than a one-time double champion could take, for wherein lay his pride? Lottie Mwale faded from public notice and, with him, went the entire sport of professional boxing from the nation's face. Frustrated, all Zambia tacitly declared professional boxing a dead sport.

But they were all wrong, for Lottie Mwale came back. With all the rubble that could be roused by one coming from the dead. 'Ladies and Gentlemen! We are pleased to inform you that boxing is still alive and kicking!'

Unbelievable. After ten solid months of hibernation, Gunduzani appeared from nowere and coolly declared, 'I am back where I started.'

As if nothing had happened, he went on training at Lusaka's Evelyn Hone College gymnasium convinced that the time had come for him to become a world champion. Thirty-four years old and unrated anywhere at all, could that be viable? What with the nearly one year of complete inactivity. 'I'm too young to resign and I'm coming back.........I am sure to get the ABU title and the Commonwealth title,' Mwale told the *Zambia Daily Mail* in March 1987 as he prepared for a catchweight fight against Zimbabwean and former African heavyweight champion, Proud Kilimanjaro, two months later in

Harare. Who could blame the people for staring at him incredulously and laughing at him under the armpits?

Absurd indeed, but did Muhammad Ali not do it twice? Or better still, George Foreman who came from a ten-year lay-off to win a heavyweight fight? What about Sugar Ray Leonard who, two months later dethroned middleweight Marvin Hagler, after a three-year retirement from boxing as a middleweight? It was especially these two last comebacks that spurred Mwale on in his ambitious campaign as he crossed over to the south to beat Kilimanjaro over ten rounds at Rufaro Stadium in Harare, Zimbabwe, on 30 May 1987 before coming back home to start from scratch.

It was difficult to imagine a former Commonwealth champion seeking to challenge for a national title all in the name of recapturing his lost glory, but Mwale was bold enough to condenscend. Besides, is it not the principle of the wise to start from the beginning and rise up through the stages?

Things could not have worked out more in favour of Mwale as he got the national light-heavyweight title without donning gloves, almost a decade after he had relinquished it to concentrate on his pursuit of international acclaim. Enock Chama, the would-be defender of the title, gave it up a little more than twenty-four hours before their fight billed for 27 June in Lusaka.

Behind a streaming Press coverage, and with so much speculative excitement from a mesmerized public, the ageless 'leopard' bared his claws once again to put his critics to shame. Whether he would make it to his goal was immaterial. The fact still remained that Lottie Mwale was the greatest boxer ever to be reared in Zambia and, surely, one of the greatest in the world. He fought some of the world's best as Saad Muhammad, Marvin Johnson, who Mwale beat at one time, became a world champion and so did Leslie Stewart who deprived him of his command in the Commonwealth. Critics at home should be made to appreciate one fact about prize-fighters if Mwale's actions are to be looked at in their proper perspective – only the great can afford to come back.

Junior lightweight John Sichula (see his ring record) was the third Zambian boxer to win, lose and regain a Commonwealth title. Patrick Mambwe was the first after beating Australian Gwyn Jones. Mambwe's career was cut short when assailants stabbed him in the eye. Mambwe was one of three champions in the stables of Gibson Nwosu, others being Yotam Kunda and Julius Luipa.

JOHN SICHULA'S PROFESSIONAL RING RECORD:

February: 1982 (Zambia) Versus Valentine Kangwa, Sichula won on points – 8th round.

May: 1982 (Zambia) Versus Leza Poko, Sichula won on knockout – 4th round.

July: Zambia Title (Zambia) Versus Dave Malo Kapili, Sichula won on TKO – 11th round

August: (Nigeria) Kabiru Akindele, Sichula won on points – 8th round

December: (Ghana) Versus Ray Akway, Sichula won on TKO – 4th round.

January: 1985 (Zimbabwe) Versus Steve Sting, Sichula won on TKO – 4th round

February: Commonwealth title (Zimbabwe) Versus Langton Tinago, sichula won on TKO – 5th round.

March: (Zambia) Versus Valentine Kangwa, Sichula won on TKO – 4th round

April: (Zimbabwe) Versus Prince Harold, Sichula won on TKO – 2nd round

September: African title (Nigeria) Versus Safiu Okebadan, Sichula won on TKO – 8th round

November: (Zambia) Versus Haste Sankisa, Sichula won on TKO – 6th round

December: (Togo) Versus Bossa Aziza, Sichula won on TKO – 6th round

April 1984:   Versus John Rubin (Uganda) Draw – 6th round

May: (Italy) Versus Hugo Carrizo, Sichula won on points – 10th round

May: Versus Belgian champion, Sichula won on TKO – 3rd round

June 1984:   (Italy) Versus Antonio Franco, Sichula won on TKO – 3rd round

August: (Portugal) Versus Franco Rhealino, Sichula won after - 3rd round

October: (USA) Versus Robert Mullins, Sichula won on TKO – 4th round

November: Commonwealth (Australia) Versus Lester Ellis – Sichula lost on points

June 1985:   (Zambia) Versus Haste Sankisa, Sichula won on TKO – 3rd round

December 1986: (Commonwealth and African titles) versus Sam Akromah Sichula lost on disputed points decision. Re-match was ordered.

CHISANDA MUTTI'S DETAILED RING RECORD

June 1980 – Chisanda Mutti thrashed Scorpion Ofusu of Ghana on a sixth round technical knockout in Lusaka in a middleweight non-title fight. Mutti won his second fight in Europe after outpointing Eddie Smith of Manchester in a non-title fight in Coventy. August – Mutti knocked out West German Light heavyweight champion Uwe Meineke in the third round of their ten-rounds fight in Cologne, Germany, November – Mutti stopped Camerounian Louis Pergaud in the fourth round in Cologne.

February 1981 – Mutti defeated substitute American Fred Brown unanimously in a non-title fight in Kiel, West Germany. Brown was knocked out by Lottie Mwale in the seventh round in 1976. April – Mutti beat Italian Cristano Cavina over ten-rounds in a light heavyweight contest in Kiel. Cavina was ranked number four in Europe when he fought Mutti. June – Mutti drew with Pablo Ramos of Puerto Rico in West Germany. The Zambian also halted former African Boxing Union (ABU) light heavyweight champion Bagayuko Sounkalo of Mali on an eighth round TKO in an ABU eliminator in Lusaka. The victory meant Mutti was to meet Lottie Mwale for the title.

May, 1982 – Mutti outpointed James Williams of the USA over ten rounds in Cologne. Williams was a last minute substitute for another American junior heavyweight Pablo Ramos. July 1982 – Mutti was stopped in the thirteenth round of the scheduled fifteen rounds bout in Lusaka. Mwale defended both the African and Commonwealth light heavyweight titles, after winning on TKO. British referee Mike Jacobs, a replacement for Roy Ankrah of Ghana, stopped the fight in the middle of the round. Mwale said after the fight: 'My punch is powerful. I could have knocked him out in the early rounds.' Mutti noted: 'I am surprised that the referee stopped the fight when I never gave in.'

In a pre-fight comment, Mutti said: 'Like Muhammad Ali when he fought his former sparring partner Larry Holmes, it is my turn to be champion after once having been Lottie's sparring partner.'

Before he fought Mwale, Mutti in twenty-five professional fights had lost twice as a middleweight, but was undefeated as a light heavyweight, reported the Zambia Daily Mail. The defeats were to Britons Frankie Lucas and Sibson in a 'Club' Middleweight fight.

April 1983 – Mutti knocked out Kid Power, alias Joseph Mutambisi, of Zimbabwe in the ninth-round of a scheduled ten rounds ABU eliminator in Lusaka.

May – Mutti beat Kid Kasempa on a TKO in the third round in Ndola to win the national light-heavyweight title.

October – Mutti unsuccessfully bid for Mwale's Commonwealth title. Mwale won on a disputed unanimous points verdict in Lusaka after twelve rounds.

November – Mutti closed the year with a third round victory over Emmanuel Owie of Nigeria (ABU elimination contest), in Lusaka. The victory propelled Mutti to meet rival Mwale for the third time.

May 1984 – Mutti drew on points with Jeff Lampkin in a ten-round light heavyweight non-title fight in West Berlin. The fight was voted 'fight of the year' in West Germany.

December – Mutti won the 'Club' cruiserweight title. He beat Stewart Lithgo of Britain into submission in the nineth round of the twelve rounds contest in Dusseldorf, West Germany.

March 1985 – Mutti beat French-based Lutshadi Mudimbi (Zaire) on points. During the same month he decisioned Tom Collins, the British cruiserweight champion on points after sending him once to the canvass in Dortmund, West Germany. By August 1985, Mutti had had thirty-one fights as a professional losing four – two to Mwale and one each to Tony Sibson and Frankie Lucas. Mutti drew twice with Jeff Lampkin and Pablos Ramos and winning the rest.

October – Mutti failed to win the International Boxing Federation (IBF) cruiserweight title from American Leroy Murphy when he was knocked out in the twelfth round.

March 1986 – Mutti was defeated in the third round by American Evander Holyfield in a non-title fight in Lancaster, Pennsylvania, USA, on a TKO.

April – Mutti earned the distinction of featuring in the 1985 IBF 'round of the year' award, the highest honour bestowed on a Zambian professional boxer. The twelfth round of his attempt for Murphy's title in October 1985 was the particular round picked by the IBF and the United States Boxing Association. He was the first Zambian to fight for an IBF championship.

May – Mutti beat Dave Russell of Australia via an eleventh round TKO in

Melbourne, Australia. Russell was ahead when Mutti's right to the head ended his hopes for Mutti's 'Club' cruiserweight crown.

Later, Mutti was knocked out in the twelfth and final round by IBF cruiserweight champion Rickey Parkey (USA) in his second attempt for the world championship in Italy. Mutti was leading on points before the TKO.

September 1987 – Mutti dethroned as Commonwealth cruiserweight champion after losing by half-a-point to Glenn McCrory on twelve rounds in London. Then he announced a shortlived retirement and bounced back in December 1987 when he lost on points to West German champion Ralf Rochiiani in Dusseldorf.

CHARM SHUFFLE CHITEULE

Chiteule started boxing in the late 1960's as a primary school pupil in Kitwe. He had many successes in the amateur ranks including the winning of two gold medals during the East and Central African Amateur boxing championships held in Tanzania in 1974 and in Zambia in 1975. Chiteule was in the Zambian boxing team enroute to the 1976 Montreal Olympic games in Canada consisting of such boxers as Lottie Mwale, John Sichula and Chisanda Mutti. 'We left for Montreal via London and had a few boxing lessons from George Francis at Highgate gymnasium in London, under the watchful eye of John Cocker. Things were not to be as expected as we watched and wondered, when we were hit by the pull-out of African countries – a boycott. Nevertheless we returned home and I started waiting for the European – Berlin championships in 1977. I thought I had won the fight against East Germany's Stefan Foster having knocked him down twice in the 2nd round. I had to settle for a bronze medal. That had to be my last fight in the amateur ranks.'

Turning professional was Chiteule's next step. He left Kitwe and hit Lusaka town hard when he joined Ronnie Sharpe's Leo Promotions. He started his professional career with six fights in 1978 – all ending in victories. Chiteule beat Patrick Mambwe, the African flyweight champion, over ten rounds and stopped Lee Graham in five rounds in Lusaka. The fight against Graham was Chiteule's first international fight as a professional. He also decisioned Zambian featherweight champion Titus Sangwapo over ten rounds.

Chiteule joined the International Sports Promotions (I.S.P.) and left with Lottie Mwale for London on 5 January, 1979 to train under George Francis. I.S.P. comprised Mr. Rupiah Bwezani Banda, Tony Phiri and Wilfried Sauerland. His Excellency Mr. Rupiah Bwezani Banda is currently the President of the Republic of Zambia.

'I must say that Boza Edwards was an inspiration during my professional career abroad,' Chiteule said.

Chiteule's first fight in Europe was against Terry McKeown in February. He knocked him out in four rounds. He later wrestled the Zambian Featherweight title from Titus Sangwapo over fifteen solid rounds in September followed by wins over Brian Snagg and Rhaman Okopoti via a second round knockout in Kitwe in November. In 1980 Chiteule was in Glasgow, Scotland, on the undercard of a world title fight between Jimmy Watt and Charlie Nash on 14 March. He fought Moroccan – Najib Daho.

'It wasn't easy to get fights in London so, Wilfried thought it wise for us to appear in shows in West Germany, United States and Zambia. And in May the same year I knocked out former British champion David Needham in five rounds in Lusaka. I closed the year with a knock out over Gerry O'Neil in five rounds in Cologne, Germany,' he said.

CHITEULE'S RING RECORD

— *1978 Versus*
Victor Mwaba – Kitwe – Chiteule won on points – six rounds
Victor Mwaba – Lusaka – Chiteule won on points – eight rounds
Patrick Mambwe – Kitwe – Chiteule won on points – ten rounds - June
Titus Sangwapo – Lusaka – Chiteule won on points – ten rounds - August
Lee Graham – Lusaka – Chiteule won on points – five rounds – November 14
Andrew Chanda – Kitwe – Chiteule won on points – ten rounds - December.

— *1979*
Terry McKeown – London – Chiteule won KO – 4th round - February 3
Toni Zeni – Lusaka – Chiteule won on points – eight rounds - March 31
Titus Sangwapo – Lusaka – Chiteule won on points – fifteen rounds - September
Chiteule won the Zambian featherweight title.
Brian Snagg – London – Chiteule won on points – six rounds – October 23
Rhaman Okopoti – Kitwe – Chiteule won on KO – second round - November

— *1980*
Najib Daho – Scotland – Chiteule lost on points – eight rounds - March 14
David Needham – Lusaka – Chiteule won on KO – fifth round – May 4, Commonwealth title eliminator.
Dieter Schantz – Cologne – Chiteule won on KO – fourth round – September 26

Zuma Grands – Lusaka – Chiteule won on KO – third round – November 1
Gerry O'Neil – Cologne – Chiteule won on KO – third round – December

— *1981*
David Greenidge – London – Chiteule won on disqualification – January 27
Potito Dimuro – Kiel – Chiteule won on points – ten rounds – February 3
Luigi Tessarin – Kiel – Chiteule won on KO – fifth round – April 10
Lloyd Allen –– Cologne Chiteule won on KO – fifth round – June 10
Samuel Meck – Lusaka – Chiteule won on points – eight round – June 28
Ray Akway – Lusaka – Chiteule won on points – eight round – September 6
Secilio Lastra – Kiel – Chiteule won on KO – second round – November 6

— *1982*
Fernadez Rodrigues – Berlin – Chiteule won on points – eight round - January 23
Nelson Azumah – Lusaka – Chiteule lost on KO – tenth round – February 28. For the African and 'Club' titles.
W.G. Sanchez – Kiel – Chiteule won on points – eighth rounds – March 26
Terry Kemp –– Cologne – Drew eight rounds – April 30
Valentine Kangwa – Lusaka – Chiteule won on points – eight round – July 4
Alberto Mercado – Las Vegas – Chiteule won on points – ten rounds – October 9
Vicho - Manheim – Chiteule won on KO – fifth round – November 13

— *1983*
Carlos Bryant – Las Vegas – Chiteule lost in round four – February 27
Rafael Jijera – Las Vegas – Chiteule won in round five – KO – May 15
Refugio Rojas – Los Angeles – Chiteule lost on points– twelve rounds – May 26
Ray Akway – Lusaka – Chiteule won on points – eight round – September 3
Robert Mullins – Frankfurt – Chiteule won on points – eight rounds – October
Barry McGuigan – Belfast – Chiteule lost on KO – tenth round – January 26
Final eliminator for the Commonwealth title
John Rubin – Berlin – Chiteule lost on points eighth round – May 25

Chiteule's instinct had told him that he went into professional boxing late. He was born on 10 October 1953. He became a professional at the age of twenty-five. And he said because of droughts, in so far as fights were concerned in England, he could not cash in as expected.

'I had always hoped that the only time I was going to earn some 'good bread' in the ring was going to come from a World Championship fight – which never came. Of course as I seemed to have missed the opportunity which presented itself at a time of not rising to the occasion. The fight game is a very physically demanding sport for I have lived probably half of my life in tip-top condition. When you are young you are bound to reach top form in a flash.

At 25 my handlers should have gambled and thrown me in fights rather than wait till late. I owe all my boxing life to Wilfried Sauerland. He tried to get me reasonable fights but it wasn't to be. May be because of the forces that be. I still feel that if I had started earlier I would have probably fulfilled my ring ambition to become a world champion.

The fight which exposed me was against Lee Graham on 14 November. I was on the undercard of the Lottie vs. Ennio Cometti fight. The Independence Stadium in Lusaka was really packed. I was still with Ronnie Sharpe so I knew that, if I had to make it in this boxing world it had to be then. I danced around Graham and shuffled to the crowd before finishing the fight in the fifth round. I knew then that I had earned myself a ticket to London, though negotiations seemed to take long. I eventually left for London in January. In 1980 when I knocked out former British Featherweight champion David Needham for what was said to be a Commonwealth eliminator, I had to wait until 28 February when I got hit by a rabbit punch from Azumah Nelson, the current world featherweight champion. It is not wise to keep on bringing excuses but certainly some cases have to be looked at from different angles. I could have put up a better fight against Azumah but I have not always seen anything special about him or may be I coudnt't rise to the occasion on that blistering 28 February afternoon. All the same, I did enjoy the fight while it lasted.

AFTER THE AZUMAH FIGHT

Chiteule said hell broke loose and wondered what was left for him in boxing. 'I could have quit the ring right there and then but since I wasn't convinced of the Azumah fight result, I thought of staying in the game for a few months or so. I hadn't made any money and it wasn't my aim that I must fight or to make some money but just for the sheer love of the game."

'Charm' was back in the ring on 26 March against W.G. Sanchez in Kiel winning on points and drawing against Terry Kemp on 30 April before returning to fight Valentine Kangwa on 4 July in Lusaka. He won on points after eight rounds.

'I went back to London for more training having been told that my next fight was going to take place in the United States. I was excited and I couldn't wait to be there. I went to Las Vegas from London just a week after the Lottie Mwale/Mustafa Muhammad fight in Las Vegas on 30 September 1982.'

Chiteule trained with Boza Edwards throughout before the fight because Edwards was also on the same bill at Show Boat Hotel. The fight was watched in other States on television. 'I sent my opponent Alberto Mercado of Pueto Rico to the canvas twice before winning on points over ten solid rounds. I made a hit in the United States of America. I came back from Las Vegas with a wide smile and knocked out a European champion Vicho in Manheim in five rounds in November 1982. I returned to Las Vegas in February of the following year and lost on a cut-eye in the 4th round to Carlos Bryant – but knocking down Rafael Jijera in five rounds on 15 May, before losing to Refugio Rojas in Los Angeles over 12 blistering rounds for the United States Junior lightweight title.'

Chiteule closed 1983 with victories over Ray Akway and Robert Mullins in Lusaka and Frankfurt respectively.

— 1984

'I looked back through the year that had passed and found out that my time in boxing was absolutely winding up therefore having been promised a final eliminator fight for the Commonwealth title against Barry McGuigan I thought that if I lost, that was definitely going to be the final curtains in as far as professional boxing was concerned for me. I had trained through Christmas time and even went to Belfast for a pre-fight build up because the fight was scheduled for 26 January 1984. Boxing is a very delicate sport – it is usually the case that your mind could be willing but your body and legs would not. I lost to Barry McGuigan on a stoppage in the 10th round. I couldn't believe the outcome, though George Francis was not in my corner—that shouldn't be an excuse.

Final Round

'Of course I had hoped to make some "good bread" out of my boxing career. But the only way I was going to make good bread was going to be via a world Championship fight and this didn't seem to come. I went to Berlin and lost an easy six rounds fight to John Rubin on 25 May 1984. I finally announced my retirement.

'I arrived home hot and cold and wondered about my future as I formed Shuffle International Promotions (SIP). I did only one show which was sponsored by a Lusaka firm. The tournament featured a local title fight between Albert Musankabala and Flywell Botha. Musankabala won. I had to abandon my promotions because of hustles from here and there. I drifted to

Kabwe Industrial Fabrics and formed a boxing club. The club is doing well. During the fourth All-Africa Games my boxer John Tayabunga won a bronze medal for Zambia.'

Figure 31: Zambia's Esther Phiri (left) dodges a punch from Kelli Cofer of the United States of America during the Women's International Boxing Federation (WIBF) Super-featherweight title fight in Nairobi, Kenya. Phiri won.

Figure 32: Esther Phiri (right), Zambia's female boxing icon, fights with Colombia's Lely Luz Florez during a light-welterweight game in Lusaka, Zambia, on 29 January 2011. Phiri won the game to unify the Women's International Boxing Association (WIBA) and Women's International Boxing Organization (WIBO) light-welterweight titles.

Figure 33: Esther Phiri of Zambia (left) lands a right punch on the face of Terri Blair of the United States of America in a Women's International Boxing Association (WIBA) Light-welterweight title fight in Lusaka on 28 November 2009. The match was a draw.

Figure 34: Zambia's All-Africa and Commonwealth light-heavyweight champion, Lottie Mwale (right) in action.

Figure 35: A hero's welcome greets heavyweight boxer Joseph Chingangu on arrival at Lusaka International Airport, Zambia.

GOLF

Golf is a game which has changed very little over a very long period. It is thus very repetitive and there are no dramatic or significant changes in the game unlike, for example, year by year improvements in world athletic and swimming records or, in recent times, improved techniques in gymnastics which have led to higher standards of performance not envisaged even ten years ago.

For the same reason the administration of golf remains largely the same from one year to another, whether in Zambia or elsewhere. Thus, it is perhaps more appropriate to catalogue development since 1964 instead of referring to achievements.

The most significant development in golf in Zambia over the past twenty-four years then had been the change in the composition of persons playing the game, bearing in mind that at Independence in 1964, there were about 3,600 male golfers and for 1985 the total is much the same according to the former Zambia Golf Union (ZGU) Secretary Owen Philips.

In 1964 and for quite a few years thereafter, the sport was almost entirely expatriate dominated in terms of the number of players and consequently in terms of golf administration. The reason was mainly historical, in that although there were obviously a number of exceptions, senior and middle positions in the Civil Service, in the armed forces, in the municipal administrations, in business, industry and farming were mainly filled by non-Zambians. Apart from what may be termed economic or social considerations, golf (and other sports such as cricket) in what is now called the Third World countries was probably regarded by the indigenous citizens as a 'whiteman's game,' in which their exposure to golf was either very limited, or the opportunities to play or to learn the game were limited.

As a result, the number of Zambians playing the game at Independence, especially those of ability to figure prominently in the Zambia Golf Union or Club Open tournaments, was only a handful. One outstanding exception at the time was David Phiri, who not long before had won his 'Blue' (University colours) while studying at Oxford, playing off a handicap of one and was soon competing successfully against the leading expatriate golfers in Zambia at that time. There were nonetheless a considerable number of Zambians who were familiar with the game. These mainly involved the caddies, comprising schoolboys or students earning pocket money or others who for want of a better education made caddying a source of livelihood.

However, by the early 1970's there had been a noticeable and welcome increase not only in the number of Zambians playing golf but also in the number of prizes won by them in competitions. This resulted from the following developments:

(a) the progressive phasing out of expatriates in the Civil Service, in the civic administrations and other sectors and the appointment of indigenous Zambians to their posts;

(b) similar changes in the business and industrial sectors, especially as a result of the economic reforms announced by President Kenneth David Kaunda which became effective from the late 1960's;

(c) as a result of a) and b), an increasing number of Zambians were able to afford the game; and

(d) the ripple effect in Zambia of the worldwide 'explosion' in the number of persons playing the game. This took place in the 1960's as a result of increased television coverage of major professional golf tournaments, substantial improvements in prize money for such tournaments and influence at that time of such megastars as Arnold Palmer (in particular), Jack Nicklaus and Gary Player. As in many other countries, these developments stimulated a considerable additional interest in the game and a large number of Zambians joined the bandwagon.

The swing in the proportion of Zambian to expatriate golfers was also reflected in the changes in golf administration in the country , both at Zambia Golf Union and at club Committee levels. However, in this case the change was more gradual, for a number of reasons. These include the fact that in any society, the percentage of persons prepared to become the work-horses for the benefit of their fellow citizens is limited. Secondly, golf is a very individualistic game. That is, it is fundamentally a game in which a player pits himself or herself against the course. Every single time a golfer starts a round of golf he or she does not know whether he or she is going to play well or otherwise, but hope springs eternal. Thus the vast majority of golfers all over the world simply want 'to get on with it,' leaving others to do the administration. Another factor underlying the desire 'to get on with it' is that the game is very complex. There are several hundred rules, with it' is that the game is very complex. There are several hundred rules, definitions and procedures governing the game and what may or may not be done in any particular situation. These rules, definitions and procedures have evolved over the last three hundred years or more, all designed to ensure that a player should not gain an unfair advantage over his fellow competitor or that he should not be unfairly treated in a given set of circumstances.

According to David I. Stirk, FRCS, the co-author of a book *The Compleat Golfer*, which is a copyright of Henderson and Stirk Limited in the United Kingdom, the origins of golf are uncertain – as uncertain as the place of its origin. The idea of hitting a ball with a stick is universal. It may be a leather ball hit with a cricket bat, a ball hit with a stick from horseback, as in polo, or it may be a ball struck on the green baize cloth with a billiard cue.

The particular form which involves hitting a stationary ball with a stick and trying to get it into a hole in the ground probably originated in Scotland. However, there are records and maps of courses in Holland dating back to the year 1926, showing a similar game to golf except that it seems to have involved hitting the ball to a target such as a church door, a tree or a castle gate.

As far as the game is concerned, one of the earliest records is contained in a royal Edict of 1457 when James, the Second, of Scotland decreed that the game be banned. This was decreed because the game of golf was so popular that it was interfering with the practice of archery. At that time archery was of great importance because it was involved in the defence of the country.

The earliest golf clubs were made entirely of wood and the balls were leather cases stuffed with boiled goose or chicken feathers. These balls were difficult to make and a good workman could only make three a day. Consequently, golf balls were very expensive, costing four to five time the cost of a club.

The first organized golf, that is Golf Clubs with properly run competitions, started in 1744 at Leith near Edinburgh in Scotland. Initially Golf Clubs were Masonic Lodges and the golf was merely a form of exercise on which they could lay bets and work up an appetite for a gargantuan dinner afterwards.

Notwithstanding the rising Zambian membership in golf clubs, for a long period the non-Zambian element remained a significant proportion (this is still the case in several golf clubs) and this was reflected in the composition of club committees elected at annual general meetings. As a result, in several clubs at least Zambian membership on club committees was less than their proportional representation of the total membership within such clubs, but this was partly also because of the factors described in the preceding paragraphs. Even so, some clubs gave early recognition to the principle of Zambian representation, a notable example being the election of Sundie Kazunga, former Zambia's ambassador to Belgium, as captain of Chainama Hills Golf Club in 1968.

During the 1970's an increasing number of Zambians were elected to serve on committees and the process continued in the 1980's to the extent where club committees were nearly all Zambian, or Zambians held many of the key positions. One interesting development in one or two clubs in recent years has been recognition among the members of the election to committee membership of 'the man for the job.' Where a committee had previously been all Zambian, in some cases non-Zambians have subsequently been elected as being the person(s) regarded as best suited for a particular position.

Having regard to the foregoing, the 1970 report of the Zambia Golf Union Executive Committee included the following statement:

> *Encouragement of Golf*
> Your executive wishes to emphasise once again that it is imperative to encourage Zambian participation in golf and golf administration. Obviously with high costs little can be done to reduce subscription rates. Moreover, it is not suggested that golf clubs should develop as purely social clubs; the main interest should be the playing of golf. However, with the greater participation of Zambians in industry and commerce, etc, there will, undoubtedly, be more candidates for membership. It is not proposed that the standards should be lowered but every assistance should be given to such candidates to become members if they can afford the expense. It is hoped that all members, expatriate and local, will be encouraged to maintain the high standards of conduct and sportsmanship for which golf is well known.

At the level of the Zambia Golf Union, the first Zambian to be elected to the Executive was Sundie Kazunga, who served from 1971-74. David Phiri joined the Executive in 1973 and served continuously until his appointment to an overseas diplomatic post in 1982. Henry Shikopa served on the Executive for three years from 1974 and Chembe Phiri joined the Executive in 1978, succeeding David Phiri as president in 1982. With the election of Pat Puta to this position in 1985, a Zambian had been president of the ZGU for the past six years then. Of the membership of the Executive, there were five Zambians and two expatriates and it may well be that from next year the Executive could be entirely Zambian.

Other developments of interest to the game of golf in Zambia and/or of its administration comprise:

The evolution of the annual 'Safari' professional golf circuit, organized under the auspices of the Professional Golfers' Association (PGA) European Tour in the United Kingdom. The circuit consists of tournaments in about March/April each year in the Ivory Coast, Nigeria, Kenya, Zambia and Zimbabwe. Ndola Golf Club was instrumental in pioneering professional golf tournaments in Zambia, the first such event- the 'Cock O' the North' – being staged in 1954 with entries primarily from professionals in central and southern Africa. For some years professional tournaments were held on an annual basis in Ndola and in Kenya. In 1969 Lusaka Golf Club staged its first tournament, followed by Mufulira in 1970. It is at that stage that the nucleus of what is now the Safari Circuit was established, with professionals from the United Kingdom and Ireland as the main source of participants, along with the then Zambian and East African professionals.

In 1977, the number of professional tournaments held in Zambia was reduced from three to two, following a request from the Professional Golfers' Association. It had been found that the earlier start to the tournaments in Europe left insufficient time for the visiting professionals to prepare themselves for these events. Between 1977 and 1985 the professional tournaments on the Copperbelt were held on a rotational basis between Ndola and Mufulira, with the other being staged at Lusaka Golf Club, which since 1979 has been the venue for the Zambia Professional Open. In 1986, it became necessary to reduce the tournaments in Zambia to one only, as a result of the introduction of the foreign exchange auction system and the major devaluation of the Zambian Kwacha against other currencies. One effect of such devaluation was the very substantial increase in the funds needed to stage the tournament. For the 1986 Zambia Open, the prize money of approximately £57,000 equated to K592, 000 and together with the expenses relating to the organization and running of the Zambia Open, funds totaling approximately K800, 000 had to be raised.

Throughout the years, the drain on Zambia's foreign exchange through payment of prize money won by the visiting professionals has been minimal, after taking into account the 30 per cent Government Entertainment Tax, entry fees payable in sterling and local spending by the visitors, plus Zambia Airways' income from the air tickets paid by the visitors in foreign currency.

The standard of organization of the tournaments in Zambia has drawn high praise from the PGA and the visiting professionals, it being held to be better than most of the professional tournaments staged in Europe. Each year the tournaments staged in Zambia have grown in popularity, there being more than 110 entries for 1986 from 11 countries. The bulk of the professionals came from the United Kingdom and Ireland, but included entries from as far afield as the United States of America and New Zealand.

Payment of Entertainment Tax to Government has over the years added up to a considerable amount and as a result golf is probably the only sport in Zambia which makes a significant contribution to Government income. For 1985, the tax paid was K63, 000 and for 1986, following the steep devaluation of the Kwacha under the auction system, the amount was nearly K178, 000.

Around 1970, Zambia's first Republican President Dr. Kenneth David Kaunda agreed to a proposal for the construction of a nine-hole course within the grounds of State House, in order to provide him with a means of relaxation from his onerous and continual responsibilities as Head of State. The 'State House Golf Club' thus came into being and, led by Dr. Kaunda who has shown himself to be a capable and consistent player, the State House team had developed an almost legendary ability to win its matches against any opposition, whether local or from overseas. The former have included several clubs affiliated to the ZGU. A considerable number of visiting and local golfers had been greatly honoured by invitations to play at State House. The opportunity afforded to meet and play golf on a regular basis with a Head of State must surely be unique in the world.

Over the years, technical and other assistance rendered by clubs affiliated to the ZGU, notably the Lusaka Golf Club had enabled the State House course to be developed to the stage where it is – in excellent condition and a fine test of golf.

In 1981, the Supreme Council for Sport in Africa decided that there should be annual competitions in various sports among the countries affiliated to the Organisation of African Unity, for which a number of regional zones were established. Zambia was allocated to Zone VI, along with Botswana, Lesotho, Malawi, Mozambique, Swaziland and Zimbabwe. The inaugural golf tournament was staged in Botswana in 1982, with Malawi acting as the host country in 1983, Zambia in 1984 and Zimbabwe in 1985. The 1986 Zone VI tournament was due to be held in Swaziland, but had to be cancelled mainly because of fund raising difficulties. The Zambia Golf Union stepped into the breach by offering to stage the 1986 tournament on the Copperbelt later in the year, a gesture which was greatly appreciated by the other Zone VI countries.

Zimbabwe won the tournament in 1982, 1983, 1985 and 1986. Zambia's team turned in a meritorious performance by winning in 1984 and the high standard of organization of the tournament won warm praise from the visitors. The rest of Zambia's record of participation was third in 1982, fifth in 1983 (a disappointing performance way below the team's potential) and second in 1985 and 1986. Zimbabwe, with more players and more golf courses that all the other Zone VI members combined, is the strongest golfing country in the region.

In 1972 the ZGU introduced a metricated Handicapping System, similar to that in use in the United States of America and in a number of other countries. Various refinements have been made over the years and if the system is applied properly, the effect is that each golfer has a handicap which is fair in relation to his ability and in relation to the handicaps of his fellow players.

In 1973, the ZGU introduced the Order of Merit system, whereby in each of the annual ZGU tournaments and Club Open competitions, the best twenty scores returned by the players are awarded points on a graduated basis. The winner and runner-up of the Order of Merit at the end of each year are awarded prizes. The Order of Merit system was designed to facilitate the selection of ZGU teams, stimulate interest in golf on a national basis and to encourage golfers in Zambia to play on as many courses as possible. All three main aims have been successfully achieved.

Over the years there were regular 'No Shows' at ZGU events or Club Opens, that is, players who had entered for a tournament but did not show up or send an apology for their inability to play and thereby causing last minute re-arrangements of the draws. The problem was dealt with by the development of a Code of Disciplinary Measures, in terms of which a 'No Show' is given a Yellow Card for a first non-appearance without apology and a Red Card status (three months' suspension from all golf) for a season. Although there are still a number of 'No shows' at tournaments each year, the Disciplinary Code has had a salutary effect.

David Phiri, an Oxford 'Blue' and a prominent golfing figure in Zambia, had the following to say:

'For many years my name has been linked with the game of golf although in my younger days I was more of a soccer player. I have dabbled in many other games too – tennis, squash, bowls and rugby for example – and I still take a keen interest in all sport. But Golf has dominated my sporting life since 1959, a long stint, and one which I intend to continue in years to come.

I started playing golf at Bristol University in England in 1959 where I was reading for a Diploma in Social Sciences. I obtained golf colours at Bristol and was selected to play for the English Universities team (excluding Oxford and Cambridge) against Scottish Universities in 1960. In September

1960, I moved to Oxford to read for a Bachelor of Letters (L. Litt) Degree and of course to continue with golf. I did obtain both a degree and a 'Blue' (the highest honour in sport at both Oxford and Cambridge). To obtain a 'Blue' you have to play for Oxford University against the traditional 'enemy,' Cambridge. I played twice in 1962 and again in 1963. In 1962 we had a historic match. The match was halved for the first time in fifty years. I was chosen to play the last of the ten singles matches. This was an honour as it meant the Captain considered me to be an 'anchor.' Before I left England I was chosen to be captain of a combined Oxford and Cambridge team which toured Scotland in April 1963.

At the end of 1963, I decided to return home. There was a lot of interest as to how I would fit in with the local golfing 'whites.' In the United Kingdom I was the only 'black' playing golf and hence I had more than my fair share of the press coverage – I was also known among my golfing friends as the 'blackman.' After protesting initially, I learnt to accept the name as some form of endearment. Some of my friends never actually got to know my proper name!

'The first game of golf I played on African soil was a Royal Salisbury in November 1963 – after the Committee had had a special meeting to discuss whether I should be allowed to play. Rumour had it that I got in by one vote, a very narrow margin. I played a four-ball which included my mentor and guardian, Philip Brownrigg, who was then head of the Anglo American Corporation in Central Africa. The Caddies at the club, now called Royal Harare, refused to caddy so that they could watch me play, and one even insisted on sheltering me from the sun with an umbrella. Admittedly, I had not seen the sun in the United Kingdom for some time! Thank God, I played well. The next day the Secretary of the club was swamped with telephone calls sarcastically asking if members could play with their 'garden boys.'

Such was the attitude of many golfers in those pre-independence days. I then moved to Lusaka at the end of 1963. My first game at Chainama Hills was with my great friend Owen Philips (popularly known as OTP in golfing circles). There was still discussion as to whether I could join a club or not, and particularly as to whether I should be allowed to use the club premises even if I was allowed to play a round of golf.

In 1964, I won the club Championship by a large margin. It was not a particularly popular win but I was waging my own 'freedom fight' since I had missed the proper struggle for independence while I was student in the United Kingdom. I had to use golf clubs to win our independence to play golf.

I was keen to be a member of Lusaka Golf Club, then dominated by white civil servants and, at that time, distinctly racial in outlook. I applied for membership and was accepted and paid my subscription by stopping order –

not quite the done thing. The question of playing in the club championship became a thorny issue amongst the members as there was a debate as to whether I was a fully paid up member or not, since I was still paying by stop order. All the same; I put my name down to play and it appeared in the draw. I was determined to win this particular competition. The opposition was stiff, but this made me even more determined. On the first day, after a round of seventy-five I was trailing by two shots behind the late John Martin and Tom Shaw, both good players. Sunday mornings always posed a problem because of late parties on Saturdays. I woke up not feeling too good, and with no inclination to play golf. You can guess the reason! I think I went round in about eighty now trailing by five shots. I must confess it was a typical windy Lusaka day – another excuse. The afternoon was calmer and I had recovered from the night before. After the first nine holes of the last round, I was only two shots behind with a score of thirty-four. News soon spread. We used to have up to hundred spectators during Club championships in those days, and the bar was always closed for the last round. On the second nine, I chipped in for an Eagle three on the tenth and took the lead, and eventually won by three shots. Thus I established my presence in golfing circles having done the 'Double,' winning both the Chainama Hills and Lusaka Club Championships in the same year. Acceptability was on its way. The Copperbelt had its own thoughts before I besieged it.

In 1965 I repeated the same 'Double' although the board at Chainama Hills says I won in 1966. I was actually a runner-up in the latter year. Chainama Hills became my home club and I thoroughly enjoyed being a member there. There were great characters like Nico Victor, Ed McMahon Bill Cobbet-Tribe, Owen Philips and others, as fellow members. Anglo American supported me during a very difficult time racially. We had an unwritten pact that they would encourage my efforts to persuade Zambians to take up the game. They even offered to build a course for the Town Council in Livingston. The Council then turned it down as a 'Colonial' game only played by David Phiri. A pity!

In 1966 I was made vice-captain of Chainama Hills Club but my training in mine management meant I had to travel a fair amount as I was Personal Assistant to the Chairman of the Group, a job I can recommend to young starters starting on their career in a large company. I used to practise every lunch hour during working days, and since work finished at 16.30 hours I could often play nine holes before dark during the week.

At Chingola I played in the last Northern Rhodesia Amateur Championship at the famous and beautiful Nchanga Golf Club. This is a tremendous course by any standards. It was a seventy-two hole event. The standard of golf then just amazed me. Such players as John Drysdale, Jackie Muir, Ken Treloar,

Dougie Tighe, Phil Dunn, Red McCabe, Peterson and Simon Hobday could have taken on any amateur team in the world. I was looked upon as an 'intruder', an 'upstart', but I held my own. Golf was of a very high standard. Among the competitors was a notorious 'mover' of the ball in the rough and even on the fairway and the greens. As a result he never had a bad lie. He went round in sixty-six but did not win the championship. Cheating never pays on the golf course.

My second tournament on the Copperbelt was the Cock O' the North at Ndola Golf Club. I had travelled in my small triumph Herald. All players were normally put up by members but while I was in the bar it became clear that no one had thought of putting me up. I gracefully retired to my trusted Triumph Herald and spent the night in the car park. Next day I had a great draw playing with Simon Hobday and Terry Westbrook. Simon travelled from Mazabuka by train with no suitcase or change of clothes, but what a player he was! I played fairly well although I found the nap on the greens a nightmare. My score of seventy-six was not disgraceful. Simon Hobday won and for the prize-giving he had to borrow a jacket to add dignity to the event.

Another event of significance was the choice of the last Northern Rhodesia team to play Southern Rhodesia for the Federal Cup. A group of twenty-four players was chosen for trials at Nkana Golf Club and I was one of them. We played a Round Robin with each player playing every other player, with points awarded for wins. I finished ninth and team of twelve was needed. Much to my amazement the president of the Northern Rhodesia Golf Union came to me and said it would be difficult to include me in the team. I was just mad. The team refused to go without me but I persuaded them to go.

I played in these trials with a wiry little 'Dutch' man called Corrie Els – he had a great sense of humour. On the first tee he presented me with a book entitled '**Teach Yourself Afrikaans.**' I needed it for the mining industry. We remained good friends until he left for South Africa.

Perhaps one of the worst racial incidents I experienced on the golf course was at Nkana Golf Club in 1966 at the Champion of Champions. I was runner-up in a very strong field and really felt good about my performance. While in the locker room, a non-player came and grabbed me and said caddies were not allowed in the locker room. My wedge was handy and I was about to deliver what could have been a regrettable 'shot' but someone caught me in time. I drove to the Guest House in disgust before prize giving and a streak of cars came there to persuade me to go back. Those were the times when I felt like packing it in. I had some supporters amongst the white golfers. John Drysdale and Jackie Muir always encouraged me to continue to struggle.

At Nchanga, one white barman refused to serve me with beer as he openly said I was not a member. After a hot day this was not the reply I expected. I dealt with him using instant justice. I grabbed a nearby beer which he had opened for another customer, shook it hard and 'hosted' him until he was drenched with beer. Pandemonium in the Club House followed.

Despite all these isolated incidents, golf has been good to me. I am a member of the prestigious Royal and Ancient Golf Club of St Andrews in Scotland. I have been president of the Zambia Golf Union and president of Lusaka Golf Club and both have haboured me as an honorary life member and in addition I am honorary vice-president of Lusaka Golf Club. I am an honorary life member of Chibuluma Golf Club and an honorary member of Chainama Hills Golf Club. Golf is a great game. From a sole 'Black' campaigner I am glad to see so many Zambians playing and running the affairs of the game.

'There are many stories I have not included here which may appear later in a different form. Zambia, hopefully, will one day produce a champion of note in the world.'

The development of junior golf (school children under the age of eighteen years) has always been one of the main aims of the ZGU Executive in office from time to time. The administration of the game at junior level is mainly in the hands of affiliated clubs. The annual ZGU junior Championship, which has been sponsored for many years by Rentokil Laboratories, is held early in January each year. In addition, the Senior Golfers' Society of Zambia performs a valuable service to golf in the country by organizing an annual tournament for school-going boys and girls, with the venue alternating between Lusaka and Chainama Hills Golf Clubs. The Senior Golfers do all the organizing and provide all the prizes out of their own pockets. The fact that the tournaments are very popular is testimony to the Seniors' hard work and generosity.

Senior Golfing Societies exist in many countries in the world. The Senior Golfers' Society of Rhodesia (Northern Branch) was formed in 1962 and it became the Senior Golfers' Society of Zambia in 1964. In line with their counterparts in other countries, the qualifying age to become a senior is fifty-five years. The total membership is limited to hundred persons and is by invitation only, in which among other considerations due regard is paid to services to golf while the player was still a 'junior.' An increasing number of indigenous Zambians are now Senior Golfers, the first to whom were Hastings Masabo of Luanshya in 1978 and David Kilisirira of Kabwe in 1979, the then President of the Republic of Zambia, Dr. Kenneth David Kaunda, was elected an honorary member of the Society in April 1979 and Party Secretary General, Mr Grey Zulu, became a senior in September 1979.

Kabwe Golf Club is the 'home Club of the Senior Golfers' Society, being the venue for the annual Seniors' Championships in April each year, followed by the annual general meeting at which the office bearers for the ensuing year are elected. Through the year the seniors play a series of matches against the various clubs affiliated to the ZGU and against the Women's Sections of several clubs, ending up with the popular match against Cainama Hills Golf Club in December and a Christmas lunch.

One of the traditions at all matches is a series of fines imposed on the Senior golfers for lighthearted misdemeanours, the proceeds from which are then handed over as a donation to the host club.

In the mid-1960's the then ZGU Executive arranged a series of annual championships for caddies, following a qualifying round at each of the clubs to determine the finalists. The arrangement included special tuition by club professionals for the more promising caddies, paid for by the ZGU, one of the objectives being that some of them could graduate to membership of the club in their area. While this happened in a number of cases, it would appear from the ZGU records of that time that some of them could not in the absence of regular employment afford the cost of membership and others simply preferred to continue caddying as a means of living.

In 1976, Colgate, Palmolive Zambia Limited developed proposals for sponsoring a National Caddies Youth Tournament, limited to those under twenty-three years of age. In terms of the procedures, a qualifying round is held at each club, from which the four best caddies within the age limit qualify for the national final. The tournament has been held annually since 1977, involving Colgate Palmolive in an outlay of many thousands of Kwacha. The company was also active in the promotion of other sports for young people, for which it is highly commended.

Various clubs annually stage a number of fund-raising tournaments for charitable organizations in the country. These are always well supported and as a result thousands of Kwacha is provided each year for the less fortunate citizens.

The Zambia Golf Union has been an affiliate member of the National Sports Council of Zambia since the latter's inception and has maintained a cordial relationship with the Council through the period concerned.

International Participation

— *1964*

Participation by a team of four players for the Eisenhower Trophy (World Amateur Team Championship) – Rome, Italy.

— *1966*

Participation in the Eisenhower Trophy Tournament – Mexico City.

— *1968*

Participation in a quadrangular tournament at Moshi, Tanzania, against Kenya, Tanzania and Uganda, won by the Zambia A team with the Zambia B team coming third. The players from Zambia also played in the Tanzania Open Amateur Championship, which was won by Harry McQuillan (Mufulira) with Simon Hobday (Chainama Hills) second and Jackie Muir (Nkana) third.

— *1970*

The intended participation by Zambia in the Eisenhower Trophy Tournament in Madrid fell through because of the presence of a team from South Africa. This had been the position ever since then.

— *1972*

Short visit by a Kenyan team in April. One match played at Lusaka Golf Club which was won by Zambia.

Participation in a second quadrangular tournament in Nairobi, which was again won by Zambia. In the Kenya amateur Singles Matchplay Championship Bob Katontoka (Chainama Hills) lost in the final to the reigning Kenyan champion, John Mucheru.

— *1973*

Tour of Zambia by the Lancashire Country team. Zambia and Lancashire each won one match, but Zambia won the inaugural trophy by winning the greater number of individual matches.

— *1974*

Participation in third quadrangular tournament in Kenya, which was won by Kenya for the first time with Zambia coming second. The Zambian team played below their normal performance level.

— *1975*

Second tour of Zambia by Lancashire. As in 1973, Zambia and Lancashire each won one match, but Zambia retained the trophy by again winning the greater number of individual matches. Results: first match Lancashire 7½ points, Zambia 5½. Second match Zambia 9½ and Lancashire 3½.

In a quadrangular tournament in Kenya, the Zambian team was unable to repeat its outstanding performance against Lancashire in Lusaka. The later won the tournament, with Kenya coming second and Zambia a disappointing third.

However, Colin van der Merwe (Nkana) won the Kenya Amateur Singles Matchplay Championship

— *1976*
Zambian team tour of Kenya and participation in the Kenya Amateur Championship. Results not on record.

— *1977*
Zambia team tour of Lancashire. Results: first match Lancashire nine points and Zambia four. Second match Zambia seven and Lancashire six. Lancashire won the trophy by winning the greater number of individual matches. To beat Lancashire on their home ground and on one of the top championship courses in the United Kingdom (Royal Lytham and St. Anne's) was a great performance.

— *1979*
Triangular match in Zambia with Kenya and Malawi, which Zambia won very easily.

Inaugural participation in international tournament (individual strokeplay) in Lubumbashi. Won by Tony McGuirk (Nkana) with players from Zambia in the next four places.

— *1980*
Zambian team tour (August/September) of Kent and Northern Ireland. Mixed performance result, mainly as a result of exhausting itinerary and foreign climatic conditions.

— *1981*
Zambia team participation (November) in the Lubumbashi International tournament. Won again by Tony McGuirk (Nkana) against very strong opposition from overseas players. Team even won by Tony McGuirk in partnership with Peter Armstrong (Chainama Hills).

— *1982*
Participation in the inaugural Supreme Council for Sport in Africa Zone VI tournament in Gaborone, Botswana. Zambia came third after Zimbabwe and Botswana.

Short visit to Harare in April. Played one match against the Zimbabwe

Golf Association, which the latter won. The team played as individuals in the Zimbabwe Amateur Open, but without success.

Reciprocal visit by Kent County team. Kent won the three match series by two to one. A triangular tournament was held at Nchanga involving Zimbabwe, Kent and Zambia, which was won by Zimbabwe.

Participation in the Lubumbashi International tournament, with Zimbabwe competing for the first time. This time Tony McGuirk finished a close second to Anderson Rusike of Zimbabwe.

— 1983

Zambia played in the Supreme Council for Sport in Africa for Zone VI tournament hosted by Malawi, but came to a disappointing fifth whereas on playing ability it should have come second or third.

The Annual Lubumbashi International tournament, in which a team from Zambia would have participated, had to be cancelled at short notice following the very substantial devaluation of the Zairean currency which made it very expensive for the hosts to stage the event.

— 1984

Zambia hosted the annual Supreme Council for Sport in Africa Zone VI tournament and emerged the winner, with Zimbabwe coming second.

Although not an 'international' event, a team of Senior Golfers from the United Kingdom toured Zambia in March/April. They were honoured by a match at State House against His Excellency's team and participated in the Senior Golfers' Society of Zambia annual championships in Kabwe.

Charlie Butts (Monze) won the Botswana Amateur Open.

— 1985

Zambia came second to Zimbabwe in the supreme Council for Sport in Africa Zone VI tournament held in Harare.

Charlie Butts (Monze) won the Botswana Amateur Open for the second time.

A four-man team participated in the Lubumbashi International tournament. Muchinga Simbule (Chainama Hills) came fourth, Labson Mbayole (Ndola) fifth, Tony Nkuwa (Nkana) seventh and George Mwanza (Nkana) eighth.

— 1986

Charlie Butts (Monze) won the Botswana Amateur Open for the third year in succession.

As noted, professional golf tournaments have been held on regular basis annually for many years. Zambia's professionals, Paul Tembo (who turned professional in August 1975), Sam Mwanza (professional in May 1976), Peter Sinyama (professional in April 1980) and Peter Armstrong (professional in November 1982) have participated in these tournaments and also in some of those staged in West and East Africa and Zimbabwe, but with limited success in terms of prize money winnings. Peter Sinyama was the professional in the team which won the British Caledonian Pro-am tournament at Gleneagles, Scotland in 1984. In November 1984, Peter Armstrong applied for reinstatement as an amateur golfer in accordance with the procedures laid down by the Royal and Ancient Golf Club of St Andrews (to which the Zambia Golf Union is affiliated) the reinstatement became effective in November 1987, the two-year minimum applicable in such in such cases. George Mwanza of Nkana Golf Club turned professional in April 1986.

The second prestigious $1 million international tournament staged by the major United Kingdom tobacco group, Dunhill, was held at St Andrews, Scotland, in September 1986. Zambia had been greatly honoured by an invitation for a three-man professional team to participate in the tournament and its representatives were Paul Tembo, Peter Sinyama and Sam Mwanza. Zambia represented the Africa region and Argentina, which also had been invited, represented the Americas. Of the other fourteen nations which participated, eight were seeded and the remaining six were determined by qualifying matches played in the Pacific region (three teams) and in Europe (three times). A team losing in the first round at St. Andrews was guaranteed US $22,500 in prize money and if it proceeded into the second round, it would earn an additional $45,000. The Zambians bowed out after losing three to zero to the USA. Tembo produced the best result among the Zambians, carding seventy-nine in the first Organisational Structure.

The Zambia Golf Union's membership is made up of clubs throughout the country, namely:

> Chainama Hills
> Chila
> Chipata
> Kabwe
> Konkola
> Lusaka
> Mazabuka
> Mufulira
> Ndola

Roan Antelope
Chibuluma
Chilanga
Choma
Kasama
Livingstone
Maamba
Monze
Nchanga
Nkana

The annual general meeting of the ZGU is held in November each year, at which the club delegates elect the Executive Committee for the following year. Clubs with a male membership of two hundred or more are allowed to be represented by two delegates and those with less than two hundred are able to send one delegate. The Executive Committee comprises the following officials:

President
Immediate Past President (ex-officio)
Vice-President North
Vice-President South
Executive Member North
Executive Member south
Secretary/Treasurer

Where the post of Secretary and Treasurer is held by separate persons then there is no election for the post of Executive Member from the region in which the Treasurer is based.

The south is defined as all clubs extending from Kabwe to the South and East of the country (therefore including Chipata) and the North comprises all clubs North of Kabwe.

Current and Past National Champions

The four major tournaments in the ZGU Fixture List are the Zambia Amateur Open (Paper Cup), the Zambia Amateur Closed (played over fifty-four holes), the Champion of Champions and the Independence Open. The most prestigious of these events is the Zambia Amateur Closed in that it carries the highest number of points for the annual Order of Merit (thirty-five to the winner as against thirty points to the winner of each of the other three tournaments).

A list of past winners of the Zambia Amateur Closed (to the extent that records are available) and a list of winners of the Order of Merit is given. By gaining the most points in the Order of Merit, which is a reflection of consistent and meritorious performance, the winner of the Order of Merit may be regarded as 'Zambia's Amateur Player of the Year.'

Instrumental Administrators

The question as to who was or has been responsible for bringing Zambian golf to where it is today is difficult to answer, simply because performance or the effect of actions taken or procedures instituted cannot be compared over a time span of twenty-four years. Perhaps an indication of those Executive members who gave or have given long periods of service to the ZGU may be of assistance.

The person who has probably made the greatest contribution to golf in the country so far is Alistair McLean. He arrived in Northern Rhodesia from Australia in 1948. Except for a gap of one year, he was president of the then Northern Rhodesia Golf Union (which changed its name to Zambia Golf Union in 1964) from 1953 to 1971. He was subsequently elected an honorary life member of the Zambia Golf Union in recognition of his conspicuous and devoted service to the administration of golf in the country.

Others with long service on the ZGU Executive are David Phiri (1974 to 1984), also an honorary life member of the ZGU), late Ernie Christian from 1966 to 1972, Nigel Pearson from 1973 to 1978, late John Dalton who was secretary/treasurer from 1973 until his untimely death in April 1980, Red McCabe from 1973 until 1982, Chembe Phiri from 1978, Owen Philips (who was president of the ZGU in 1976, 1977 and 1978 and has served as secretary/ treasurer since April 1980 and Richard Bryan from 1977 to 1985. Of the ZGU Executive then, the longest serving members, included the President, Pat Puta, who had served since 1983, and the Executive member North, Graham Roberts, who had served since 1982.

Problems

The problems/areas of concern relate to the following

— *Coaching*

At the time of Independence and until about the mid-1970's, there were a number of expatriate professionals attached to various clubs in the country. It should be noted that an important source of income for coaching professionals (that is those who are not mainly dependent on earning a living through prize money won by competing in tournaments) is the profit made from sales of golf equipment to club members. As a result of the economic problems which developed in the country some twelve years or so years ago (at the time) it became increasingly difficult for professionals to secure supplies of equipment and the expatriate professionals gradually departed to other countries.

Although the Midlands area was served by Paul Tembo and Sam Mwanza at Lusaka and Peter Sinyama at Chainama Hills (and until not so long ago by Jeanie Owens at Kabwe) the Copperbelt has had no one available for coaching for many years. This is an important gap, especially in developing the full potential of the upcoming young Zambians. The ZGU has over several years attempted to procure the services of a professional from overseas for location on the Copperbelt. Because of the high cost, such attempts have been on a joint financing basis with local companies, but these have not been successful.

With few exceptions, members of ZGU teams over a considerable number of years have been players who are no longer in their youth, examples being Labson Mbayole, Patwell Sikelo, Roger Sichone and Muchinga Simbule. Among the younger generation, only Charlie Butts and George Mwanza (who recently turned professional) have come through to the top. The ZGU Executive has for many years urged clubs to get their Zambian members to interest their children in golf. There are signs of more and more Zambian youngsters turning to the game and it is hoped that many of them will develop into future champions. For the time being, however, reliance on the 'old guards' will still be necessary.

— *Plant and Machinery*

The maintenance of golf courses to acceptable standards requires a wide variety of equipment. Apart from tractors as work-horses, these include rough cutters, fairway cutters, tee cutters and green mowers, all of which are specialized for the particular operation involved. Borehole equipment and pumps are another important feature.

The cost of all such equipment has grown markedly over the years especially after the introduction of the Bank of Zambia system of auctioning foreign exchange and the steep devaluation of the Kwacha.

Spare parts for equipment have also not been easy to come by. They are expensive and charges for repairs by local firms are also very high.

In the current circumstances, affiliated clubs are finding it very difficult to afford the cost either of procuring new machinery or maintaining it. It seems probable that many of them will have to raise membership fees or adopt other fund-raising measures. While higher membership dues are unsatisfactory in themselves and particularly from the point of view of the many Zambian players, it should be noted that in comparison with overseas clubs, the cost of playing golf in Zambia is still relatively cheap.

— *Equipment*

There have, for a number of years only, been sporadic imports of golf equipment into the country. Certain business concerns have managed to do so, but supplies have generally been limited (affecting other sports as well) and there are perennial shortages. The import of equipment in 1985 by the National Sports Council of Zambia, for golf and for other sports, was a most welcome development. Under the auction system, individual associations affiliated to the National Sports Council were free to arrange their own imports and obtain the foreign exchange by bidding under the auction system. The ZGU hoped to secure supplies of equipment through this route, for onpassing to clubs at no mark-up, but it will nevertheless be an expensive operation. The extent of any such imports depended on the ability of the affiliated clubs (and through them their members) to afford the supplies obtained externally.

— *Golf Decline*

It is presumed that the question relates to playing standards. An effective answer would only be possible by means of a detailed comparison of winning scores over say the last twenty years, for which records are not available. By good fortune, there is a list of the various tournament winners and their scores in 1963. The latter show that on several occasions the scores were lower than those currently returned by the winners of the tournaments today, but the following factors need to be taken into account:

- the winners of those days were younger people; and

- taking one set of results is an isolated example, thus in recent years the winning scores in some tournaments by Zambian players have on occasion been just as good.

Perhaps the one comment that can be made is that the current leading players in the country are not consistent enough. That is to say, in one tournament they return a reasonably good score but over the whole golfing season the number of poor scores returned is rather higher than it should be. A consistent player is one who has an occasional very good round of golf, a considerable number within striking distance of what may be expected from his playing ability and, as is only human, only a relatively few bad scores through the year.

If the question also relates to golf administration, the level of efficiency at ZGU Executive and club level is probably not all that different from say twenty years ago. A minute from an Executive meeting of that time records a complaint about various clubs not responding to questions or directives issued to affiliated clubs by the Executive. The same situation exists from time to time even today. In some clubs in recent years there has been a slight dip now and then in the organization of tournaments or in the general administration, which was probably also the case twenty years ago, or whenever.

On the brighter side, there has been a steady increase in the number of Zambians on committees. Some have turned in very good performances. The important aspect is that the proportion of Zambians who have gained or are gaining experience in all aspects of golf is growing all the time, which can only be of benefit in the future.

— *Zambian Standards Performance*
A reasonable comparison with standards abroad is not possible because of the limited competitive opportunities. At best one could describe a ZGU team which in good form is capable of giving many of the United Kingdom country teams a good run for their money. It must be noted that Zambia's golfing population is tiny compared to that of many other countries. The bigger the number of golfers in any country (as is the case with other sports) the more competition there is at the top for a limited number of positions and the greater the likelihood of a higher standard of play.

— *Zambia Amateur Closed Championship*

1973	Harry McQuillan (Mufulira)
1974	Dave Rigby (Ndola)
1975	Paul Tembo (Lusaka)
1976	Mike Wallace (Nkana)
1977	Colin van der Merwe (Nkana)
1978	Colin van der Merwe
1979	Tony McGuirk (Nkana)
1980	Colin van der Merwe
1981	Peter Armstrong (Chainama Hills)
1982	Tony McGuirk
1983	Anthony Whitty (Mufulira)
1984	Labson Mbayole (Ndola)
1985	Dudley Sammons (Mufulira)
1986	Paul Lindley (Lusaka)

— *Order of Merit*

1973	Dave Rigby (Ndola)
1974	Dave Rigby
1975	Paul Tembo (Lusaka)
1976	Peter Armstrong (Chainama Hills)
1977	Dave Rigby
1978	Peter Armstrong
1979	Peter Armstrong
1980	Peter Armstrong
1981	Colin van der Merwe (Nkana)
1982	Tony McGuirk (Nkana)
1983	Roger Sichone (Nchanga)
1984	Muchinga Simbule (Chainama Hills)
1985	Muchinga Simbule

Women's Golf

The Zambia Ladies' Golf Union was formed on 26 June, 1964 when it broke away from the rest of Southern Africa for political and ethical reasons and became directly affiliated to the Ladies' Golf Union of the United Kingdom.

Since then, the women's golf in Zambia has grown from strength to strength and although the numbers are relatively small compared to other sporting bodies in the country, the ZLGU is an active and competitive organization.

It was not until 1965 that women's golf in Zambia began to look further afield for international competitive competition and since then links have been formed with many countries – notably India, Dubai, Kenya, Nigeria, Swaziland, Mauritius, Malawi, Botswana, Uganda and Zimbabwe.

In 1966, Zambia' first team travelled to Kenya and since then strong competitive ties have been made. Kenya returned to Zambia in 1968 – the tour so strenuous it was recorded that players played three hundred holes of golf and walked some three hundreds miles, doing so all in twelve days!

This link with Kenya was the foundation of the Gilberson and Page Triangular Matchplay event which now includes Zimbabwe, and is competed for annually, each country taking the turn to host the event. At the time the holders of the Gilberson and Page Trophy were Zimbabwe. Zambia won it in 1981 and Kenya last won it in 1984.

It is hoped that the future may see an All-Africa Ladies' Open Championship with participants from All-Africa independent countries. However, the problems such as communication and expensive travel limit the possibility of this becoming a reality in the near future.

Six national fixtures are competed for annually within the country. These are:

- the Zambia Ladies' Open Amateur Strokeplay Championships;
- the Zambia Ladies' Open Matchplay Championships;
- the Northern Areas Open Ladies' Championships; and
- the Southern Areas Open Ladies' Championship.

There are also two Club Open tournaments chosen each year, all of which are elements of the Order of Merit from which are selected the players who will represent the

Zambia Ladies' Golf Union in teams to play against other countries at home and abroad.

The following are the Zambia Ladies' Golf Champions since 1962:

1962	E. Carty
1963	Pam Long
1964	Pam Long
1965	Pam Long
1966	M. McDougall
1967	Beryl Acton
1968	Beryl Acton
1969	Joan Botha
1970	Lesley Dwyer
1971	R. Lowry (Kenya)
1972	Carol Charbonnier
1973	Carol Charbonnier – later turned professional.
1974	Teresa Taylor
1975	Pat Fairlie
1976	Teresa Taylor
1977	Teresa Taylor
1978	Teresa Taylor
1979	P. Pyle
1980	Madelyn le Roux
1981	Madelyn le Roux
1982	P. Pyle
1983	Vivian Browning (Zimbabwe)
1984	Nora Jordan

1985   Jennifer Aoka (Kenya)

Nineteen eighty-four saw the tragic death of Cynthia Howell in a car accident on the eve of the Zambia Ladies' Amateur Open Championships played at Chainama Hills Golf Club. The death of Cynthia was a great loss to the women's golf in Zambia, in just the same way as when the nation loses its best women golfers because they leave Zambia to settle elsewhere. Of those listed, only Nora Jordan, a Zambian, remained in the country.

Zambia's prominent players of low handicap were:

Lilian Dunn (Roan Antelope)
Trish Houston (Konkola)
Sue McManus (Roan Antelope)
Nora Jordan (Chainama Hills)
Mary Bourne (Chainama Hills)

These golfers have all at one time or another won their own Club Championships and have been a winner or runner up in the Zambia Ladies' Open Championships. The holder of the Championship Trophy was Linda Turnbull of Zimbabwe.

Teresa Taylor who left Zambia in 1983, was perhaps our most notable woman golfer in recent years, having won at some time or another all the Zambia Club Ladies' Championships, the Zambia Ladies' Open Championships as well as those of Malawi, Botswana and Kenya. Teresa now lives in Gaborone, Botswana.

The Zambia Ladies' Golf Union has always been administered by an Executive Committee consisting of a president, vice-president South, vice-president North, executive member, secretary and treasurer, whose main duty it is to advise and further the interests of women's golf in Zambia.

Generally the Union's problems are much the same as those experienced by other sporting organizations in Zambia, such as lack of funds, unavailability of equipment which is also very expensive, profefessional guidance and coaching. However, the ZLGU is an enthusiastic and active orgnization consisting of some three hundred female playing members with registered handicaps. Most golf clubs in Zambia have active women's sections which contribute a great deal to the general running of the club as well as organizing competitions and golf clinics whenever possible for beginners and juniors.

It is encouraging to see Zambian women take up the sport and do very well as the future of women's golf in Zambia depends on them. Unfortunately one of the major drawbacks is that golf is a time consuming game and most women are wives and mothers with little time to spare and if one's husband does not play then it is very difficult for one to understand the attractions of the game.

Women's golf in Zambia has declined only because there are fewer women playing golf now. The standard is still very high, but compared to the previous years, there are fewer golfers especially in the lower handicap range – even so, they are still able to compete successfully on an international level.

Prospects for the future are not too bright unless more of the Zambian girls and women take up golf and continue to be interested enough in the sport to bring themselves up to international standards and get involved in their club's administration, learning as much as possible the technicalities of the game. Unless this is achieved in the near future, the future of women's golf in Zambia would be very bleak indeed.

Zambia won the Gilberson and Page Trophy in its early days, but has lost the trophy to Kenya and Zimbabwe. The Zambia Ladies Club Opens provide some very good competition and good golf is played – the champions are worthy champions.

Women's golf was introduced in Zambia as soon as the first golf course was constructed, if facts are correct, the Kabwe (then Broken Hill) golf course some sixty years or so ago. The records go back to 1961, but women were certainly playing golf in Zambia long before that time. As Kabwe was the first golf course to be constructed in Zambia, it too saw our first Zambian Woman Captain in Judy Mweemba and now has a full Zambian women's committee and it is on women such as these that the long term future of women's golf in Zambia depends. Most women's sections are administered by expatriates who will eventually leave Zambia to return to their homes, but they have a great deal of experience and administrative ability to impart to those interested to learn.

At the first dawn of this book the following was the Executive Committee following the departure of Pauline Dunn and the resignation of Nel Cornelius:

President	Pam Barker (Lusaka)
Vice-President	Gill Evans (Mufulira)
Vice-President North	Sue McManus (Luanshya)
Vice-President South	Mary Bourne (Lusaka)
Executive Member	Freda Heygate (Nchanga)
Secretary	Tina Ship (Lusaka)
Treasury	Nadine Barkley (Lusaka)

Figure 36: Zambian golfer Madaliso Muthiya ponders his next move.

PAST WINNERS OF ROTHMANS OF PALL MALL (ZAMBIA) ANNUAL SPORTING AWARDS

— *Sportsman of the Year*

1964	-	Samuel 'Zoom' Ndhlovu (soccer)
1965	-	Jackson Mambwe (boxing)
1966	-	Howard Mwikuta (soccer)
1967	-	Barry Dodd (athletics)
1968	-	Douglas Sinkala (athletics)
1969	-	Boniface Simutowe (soccer)
1970	-	Julius Luipa (boxing)
1971	-	Peter Mhango (soccer)
1972	-	Satwant Singh (motor sport)
1973	-	Timothy Feruka (boxing) and Dickson Makwaza (soccer)
1974	-	Emmanuel Mwape (soccer)
1975	-	Dick Chama (soccer)
1976	-	Patrick Mambwe (boxing)
1977	-	Godfrey Chitalu (soccer)
1978	-	Lottie Mwale (boxing)
1979	-	Bill Bourne (cricket)
1980	-	Peter Armstrong (golf)
1981	-	Fred Kangwa (lawn tennis)
1982	-	Peter Kaumba (soccer)
1983	-	John Sichula (boxing)
1984	-	Keith 'Spinks' Mwila (boxing)
1985	-	Efford Chabala (soccer)
1986	-	Simon Gondwe (squash)
1987	-	Satwant Singh (motor sport)

— *Sportswoman of the Year*

1970	-	Merl Moult (badminton)
1971	-	Audrey Chikani (athletics)
1972	-	Grace Munene (athletics)
1973	-	Glynis Clark (swimming)
1974	-	Phillipa Bowen (horse show jumping)

1975	-	Christine Nyahoda (badminton)
1976	-	Carol Mumbi (athletics)
1977	-	Christine Nyahoda (badminton)
1978	-	Joyce Maycock (squash)
1979	-	Joyce Maycock (squash)
1980	-	Veronica Zulu (lawn tennis)
1981	-	Madelyne le Roux (golf)
1982	-	Madhavi Tijoriwala (badminton)
1983	-	Jenny Parker (squash)
1984	-	Hilda Edwards (squash)
1985	-	Litah Muluka (athletics)
1986	-	Hilda Edwards (squash)
1987	-	Martha Lungu (athletics)

— *Sports Administrator of the Year*

1968	-	Albert Musakanya (soccer)
1969	-	None
1970	-	Tom Mtine (soccer)
1971	-	Late Eliya Mwanza (soccer)
1972	-	Stan Smith (athletics)
1973	-	Ante Buselic (soccer)
1974	-	General Kingsley Chinkuli (soccer)
1975	-	Charles Madondo (weightlifting)
1976	-	Geoff Cole (cycling)
1977	-	Ernest Mate (boxing)
1978	-	Maxwell Sichula (lawn tennis)
1979	-	late Archie Phiri (boxing)
1980	-	late Flo Morgan (hockey)
1981	-	Maxwell Sichula (lawn tennis)
1982	-	late Flo Morgan (hockey)
1983	-	Bill Chanda (boxing)
1984	-	Dino Giuseppin (cycling)
1985	-	Sarah Mulyata (netball)
1986	-	Pat Puta (golf)
1987	-	Moses Mulenga (lawn tennis)

INDEX

Soccer

Cricket

Miller, Ian 67
Millers, the 65
Murray, Jackie 65
Oates, Cedric 65
Page, Des 65
Patel, Nittin 67
Potgieter, J.J. 65
Potgieter, Monty 65
Ranchod, R. 66
Rixon, Ralph 65
Stimmel, Harley 66
Stubbs, C. 65, 66
Stubbs, John 66, 67
Stubbs, the 65
Taylor, Paul 66, 67
Turle, Gillies 67
Vaughan, James 66
Warren, Ric 67
Welker, Buzz 66
Zunkel, Bill 65

Table Tennis

Azcuy, Isaac 71
Barta, Vladimir 71
Batchelor, Ken 71
Chibwe, Charles 71, 72
Choopa, Chiwale 72
Cummings, Dave 70, 71
Daka, Alfred 72
Doki, Y. 70
Elnajaar, Squir 71
Featherstone, Keith 70
Hamaiko, George 71
Hamunyumbwe, Amos 71
Harrington Brothers of Senanga 73
Herman, Gunter 70
Higashi, Y. 70
Imwinji, Kenneth 73
Jackson, T. 71
Jumbe, Wilson 71, 72
Kaishe, Henry 71, 72
Kalumba, Felix 72
Kalwizhi, Alick 73, 74
Kano, Jigoro, Professor 69, 70
Kauta, Rick 73

Kayoya, David 71
Kim, D.S. 73
King, Don 71
Lee, Bruce 69
Long, Denis 70
Luanga, Paul 71, 72, 73, 75
Macker, Bashier 71
Mafuta, James 73, 74
Malambo, Moses 71, 72
Manda, Stephen 72
Mbewe, Boniface 74
McKenna, Jude, Fr. 70, 71, 72, 73, 75
Mukanga, Aggrey 71, 72
Mukubesa, Spencer 71, 73
Munakatesho, Donald 71, 72
Must, Len 70
Mwala, Fred 73
Mwalongo, Jerome 72
Mwanza, Francis 71
Nayee, J.R. 73
Ngoma, James 72
Ngongolo, Griffiths 73, 74
Nkamdem, Maurice 71
Okada, O. 70
Oliver, Roby 71
Peters, Tony 70, 71
Pumulo, Herbert 73, 74
Rogerson, Steve 71
Sasaki, H. 70
Shamboko, John 71, 72, 73
Sichalwe, Henry 71, 72, 73, 74
Tembo, Asaph 72, 73
Thompson, Alec 70
Walla, Robert van de 71
Yamboto, Nyambe 72
Young, Michael 71

Lawn Tennis

Aasen, Ragnar 77
Bwalya, Albert 77, 79
Bwalya, Joel 77
Cardoso, Brian 76, 79
Chanda, Peter 77
Chapman, Warwick 81
Crane, Phillip 77

Dudhia, Abdul 76
Gallagher, Sean 77
Gaunt, Harry 77, 78
Gill, Roger 76, 77
Godfrey, Peter 77
Henegan 76
Hollies 76
Kalumbe, Peter 77
Kasama, Samuel 76, 77, 78, 79
Kosoko, Tony 76
Moseley, Duncan 76
Mumba, Bentley 77, 78
Mwale, Bongo 76, 77, 78, 79
Mwandila, Victor 76, 78
Mwape, Benson 77, 79
Pitts, Clive 77, 78
Quadros, Oscar 76, 77, 78
Ryan, Brian 76, 77
Sikanyika, Mathews 77, 78, 79
Sondashi, Misheck 77

Squash

Abe, Peter 83, 85
Arichandran, K. 83, 84
Bailey, Ralph 85
Bailey, Renee 84, 85
Dunphy, Diedre 83
Howard, Jenny 83
Hudak, F 83
Jacobs, Cecil 83, 85
Jamieson, Norma 81, 83
Jokinnen 84
Kangwa, Fred 82, 83, 205
Kangwa, Patrick 82, 83
Kangwa, Steven 82, 83
King, Alan 83
Lunoe, Bjorn 81
Maibwe, Nora 83
Meleki, Douglas 81
Mibenge, Benjamin 81
Mpheneka, Dick 81, 82, 83
Mpheneka, Veronica 83
Mulenga, Billy 81
Mumba, Douglas 82
Mumba, Godwin 81, 83

Mutale, David 82
Nell, Chris 81, 85
Nichols, Ian 81, 84
Njovu, Mambo 82, 83
Patel, Solly 81, 82, 83
Ross, Clive 81, 83
Sharp, Ian 81
Ship, Tina 81, 83
Sichula, Maxwell 81, 84, 206
Simunyola, Kela 82, 83
Stokke, Egil 81, 83
Zengeni, Andrew 81

Bowls

Andersen, Lars 92, 93
Apple, Gavin 90
Balshaw, Heather 93
Banda, Mark 90
Banda, Recreena 90
Barret, Mike 92
Belshaw, Colin 93
Champo, Nick 90
Charge, Peter 90, 92
Chikani, Audrey 91
Chola, Judith 90
Coy, Davy 90
Dickenson, Tricia 92
Dunphy, Barry 90
Edwards, Hilda 90, 91, 92, 93, 206
Ferreira, Charles 90
Gondwe, Simon 90, 91, 93, 205
Gul, Fathim 92
Harvey, Neil 93
Hunter, Storr 90
Johnson, Harry 90
Kabwe, Mike 91
Kapwasha, Willie 90
Kaunda, Waza 81
Kayange, Ceaser 90
Kayula, Fidelis 91
Langston, Maggie 92
Lungu, Martha 91, 206
Machamanda, Alex 92
Malik, Ali 92
Masson, Crawford 93

Motor Sport

Athletics

Wrestling

Badminton

Boxing

Golf